*f*P

Wealth Watchers

A SIMPLE PROGRAM TO HELP YOU
SPEND LESS AND SAVE MORE

Alice Wood

with Glenn Rifkin

FREE PRESS

New York   London   Toronto   Sydney

FREE PRESS
A Division of Simon & Schuster, Inc.
1230 Avenue of the Americas
New York, NY 10020

First Free Press hardcover edition January 2010

FREE PRESS and colophon are trademarks of Simon & Schuster, Inc.

For information about special discounts for bulk purchases, please contact Simon & Schuster Special Sales at 1-866-506-1949 or business@simonandschuster.com.

The Simon & Schuster Speakers Bureau can bring authors to your live event. For more information or to book an event contact the Simon & Schuster Speakers Bureau at 1-866-248-3049 or visit our website at www.simonspeakers.com.

Manufactured in the United States of America

1   3   5   7   9   10   8   6   4   2

Library of Congress Cataloging-in-Publication Data
Wood, Alice (Alice M.).
Wealth watchers: a simple program to help you spend less and save more /
Alice Wood with Glenn Rifkin.
p. cm.
1. Finance, Personal—United States—Planning. 2. Finance, Personal—
United States—Popular works. 3. Discretionary income—United States.
I. Rifkin, Glenn. II. Title.
HG179.W5772 2010
332.024—dc22   2009023793
ISBN 978-1-4391-5819-7
ISBN 978-1-4391-7571-2 (ebook)

NOTE TO READERS

The names and identifying details of some of the people portrayed in this book have been changed.

This book is dedicated
to everyone who spends money.

CONTENTS

ACKNOWLEDGMENTS

It takes a village to start a movement and it takes a village to write a book. Thank you to the hundreds of teachers, students, bankers, government employees, business advisers, and individuals who have made this possible.

A special thanks to Mary Kay Clinton for encouraging me to write this book; to Laurie Delande, Floris Julien and George Wood for helping to create the Wealth Watchers® program; to Donna Levigne for sharing her vision that "this will be huge"; to Michael McMullen who encouraged me to "go for it"; to Shirley Bauman of the Naperville Women's Club who encouraged me not to give up, that I was really on to something; to Stephanie Penick and Positively Naperville for all of the great coverage; to Maggie Strevell of Naper Solutions who brought our message to the World Wide Web; to Liz Spencer and everyone at NCTV 17 for bringing our message to television; to Phil Gresh for introducing me to Deb Gardner who laid much of the groundwork for making Wealth Watchers a reality; to Brandon Bieber and Eddie Sandrick, our first sales reps, who worked for practically nothing because they believed in the mission; to Bill Bartlett, of Corporate Strategies and Solutions as well as Kathi Neuman and Tom Wojcik who shared their corporate experience in an attempt to get our small company ready for the big time; to Jane Shuman who brought her enthusiasm for making a difference into our early Wealth Watchers meetings; to Barb Dwyer for all of her encouragement and advice; to Loretta Wilger Asmus of Looks and Jen Bonelli of Shear Brilliance for making me "camera ready." To Ray Kinney, Kathleen Dorn, and Paula Rhodes from Minute Man Press for helping us produce the earliest versions of the Wealth Watchers journals; to Tom McInerney and Palmer Printing for refining and improving the design of our product line; to Mike McQuaid for his brilliant design work; to Dr. Alan Leis and CUSD 203 for bringing Wealth Watchers into the classroom; to Helen Hammond Redding of Citi for introducing our program to the Chicago Public Schools; to Dr. Sandra Gill and Professor Vicki Jobst of Benedictine University for bringing Wealth Watchers to college students; to Jason Alderman and everyone at Visa for putting us on the map; to Phil Watson and Cathryn Cole of Ameriprise for introducing our program to McDonald's; to Kim Appleberg and all of the great people at McDonald's USA for taking a chance on a small startup company; to Angie Neuman and everyone at US Bank for supporting our work; to everyone at The Federal Reserve Bank of Chicago for paving the way for financial literacy to become a household word; to the many men and women in Washington, DC and around the country working to bring meaningful change to the financial lives of millions of Americans.

And a special thanks to everyone who lent me money to get the Wealth Watchers project off the ground—US Bank, Harris Bank, Bank of America, Wells Fargo, American Express, Chase, Citi, Discover; and my husband, Dan McQuaid, for letting me use his ability to borrow money when mine ran out.

To Ron Nyberg and Gerry Cassioppi of Nyberg & Cassioppi for giving me the gift of time so I could concentrate on Wealth Watchers.

I'd also like to thank Joel Gotler for introducing me to one of the finest literary attorneys in the country, Frank Curtis. And a special thanks to Frank Curtis for introducing me to Steve Hanselman and Julia Serebrinsky of Level 5 Media who thankfully took a chance on an unknown author. To the entire team at Free Press/Simon & Schuster for believing in our mission to change the way the world looks at money, especially Martha Levin, Hilary Redmon, Suzanne Donahue, Heidi Metcalfe, Carisa Hays, Sydney Tanigawa, Will Prince, Erich Hobbing, Edith Lewis, and Jennifer Weidman.

A special thanks to my writing partner, Glenn Rifkin. Glenn never stopped challenging me to make the book better; the experience wasn't painless but he was brilliant to work with and I've come to think of him as a brother.

I'd like to thank all of the doctors and their staff who have helped with my recovery: Dr. Jim Collins; Dr. Preston Harley; Dr. Ricardo Senno; Dr. Michael Berkowicz; Dr. Gouri Chaudhuri; Dr. Nelson Escobar and Dr. Neil Margolis.

Lastly, I'm thankful for the support I've received from my entire family. My husband, Dan McQuaid, and my children, Eddie, Andy, and KC who are probably scarred for life because I spend so much time talking about money. My brothers and sisters who have always been there for me, especially my brother George who has saved me more times than I can count. My mom, Doris Wood, who has been part of Wealth Watchers since day one. I don't know where I would be without her. And I'd like to thank my dad, Warren Wood. Even though he's been gone for more than twenty years, he is still so much a part of this project. He taught us all that we couldn't lose if we had faith, courage, and enthusiasm.

PART I

CHAPTER ONE

A Simple Idea
with a Potent Payoff

I started Wealth Watchers in 2002 on a shoestring budget and with a deep belief in the concept. Just two years earlier, a bizarre incident on an airplane left me with a brain injury that forced me to start key parts of my life over from scratch. Where once I had been adept at handling my finances, I was suddenly like a child learning to ride a bicycle for the first time. This firsthand struggle gave me a new appreciation for how hard it can be to manage money, and what I learned along the way to my recovery inspired me to create Wealth Watchers.

At the beginning, I endured more meetings than I care to remember where the only attendees were me and a small group of friends and family members. But steadily, in surprising ways, the idea took off and gained enough traction to prove that my faith was justified. What began as a personal mission has become a movement touching many hundreds of thousands of lives.

My book is a product of this movement and is meant to offer you a financial lifeline in our troubled times. All meaningful change is personal, and my hope is that this book will serve as a powerful introduction to a system *that can and will change your financial life*. In *Jerry Maguire*, one of my favorite movies, the obstinate football star Rod Tidwell, played wonderfully by Cuba Gooding, Jr., tells his agent Jerry Maguire, "Some dudes have the coin, but they'll never have the *kwan*!" Tidwell explains that kwan means money but also love, respect, and community. It's a *package* that makes life fulfilling and worth living. Money alone can't buy it. I've come to believe that real wealth is about the whole package: financial security, integrity, love, family, thrift . . . the kwan. For me, Wealth Watchers is about the whole package.

If you follow the principles and use the tools of Wealth Watchers, you will be able to have and enjoy the things that you want no matter what your income may be. I think you will relate to the stories of people who have struggled with their financial health and be inspired by the stories of the individuals who have followed the program and fulfilled their financial goals and dreams.

This isn't a magic bullet or a get-rich-quick scheme. For me, the elegance of Wealth Watchers is in its simplicity and practicality. Our world has grown so large and complex that we are often overwhelmed by all the technology and media bombarding us. The endless flood of often misleading financial offerings, from credit products to untenable mortgages, has set off an unprecedented wave of financial disaster for naïve consumers. I can't tell you how important it is for all of us to remember that we are now living in a world of Borrower Beware.

I grew up the daughter of a bank president in Naperville, Illinois, the same Chicago suburb where I continue to live. My father was a banker in a time when community banks really cared about the success of their customers and made their money by making successful loans and investing conservatively. My father's approach had a big impact on me. I know there is no shortage of similar people in banking, even today, with strong ethics, who care deeply about their customers' success.

But what we've seen in recent years is that many of their

employers are giant banking institutions that became unrecognizable in the deregulated free-for-all that has characterized the last decade. They seem to have "evil geniuses" working in their backrooms creating new ways to generate revenues from fees and penalties from the legions of customers who never read the small print. I constantly hear stories from students who have been hit with overdraft fees because they make the mistake of assuming that the balance shown on their ATM statement is correct. It's especially ironic that debit cards were originally introduced into the marketplace to protect people from getting hit with overdraft fees because they wouldn't be allowed to purchase an item if it would cause an overdraft. But somewhere along the line, it became a "courtesy" to honor the purchase, even if that meant someone could be hit with astronomically high overdraft fees. Ugh!

Part of my mission is to energize people to ask questions, insist on answers, and perhaps move the bankers to rethink the products they offer. This all makes me think of those old Smith Barney television commercials with the actor John Houseman who stares intensely into the camera and says, "At Smith Barney, we make money the old-fashioned way . . . we EARN it!!" Wouldn't it be wonderful if we could go back to the days when banks made profits based on solid loans and investments?

My career as an estate planning attorney has provided me with a close look at people's financial lives. I've represented more than a thousand families who have had every kind of advantage and every kind of setback. Most of my clients are financially informed. But it's surprising that so many have adult children who are terrible with money. I think that disconnect comes from a monumental gap in financial education. A vast majority of states in our country do not require any form of financial education in the classroom. How sad, since many parents feel ill equipped to teach financial education at home. I look at our older clients who are above average at managing their money. They wouldn't have thought to teach their children to stay away from mortgages they couldn't afford because they were still operating under the old rules of banking in which someone had to genuinely qualify for a loan. By the time they found out their children were in over their heads with unaffordable mortgages, it was too late to undo the damage. And most of our older clients wouldn't have dreamed that their adult children would accumulate massive credit card debt. Again, by the time they discovered their children were on the verge of bankruptcy, it was too late.

As you can tell, I'm passionate about education—especially since my husband is a high school teacher. And I don't dream small dreams. I want Wealth Watchers to set off a *global* movement, creating a generation of informed and disciplined consumers who use these principles to build a financially stable and fulfilling life for themselves and their families. I want Wealth Watchers to get passed along, for us to teach its principles to our children and for our children to teach their children.

They say that timing is everything in life. I am reasonably certain that there hasn't been a better time in recent memory for a book like Wealth Watchers. When times are flush and the money is flowing, either through real earned income or wagonloads of credit, people tend to throw caution to the wind and forget about financial discipline. Let's face it, we Americans love our credit cards, believe shopping is a birthright, and don't pay a whole lot of attention to saving our money. But sometimes, we get a collective wake-up call that hits us like a bucket of ice water. And the most recent bucket has been very cold indeed. You don't need me to provide a litany of the causes of America's recent hard times. But a few facts will help establish what we've had to confront as a nation.

Less is more . . . and it's less expensive.

As I write this, America is facing its worst financial crisis since the Great Depression. Since late 2007, we have watched our collective financial well-being take a beating as a severe recession settled into place. Here are some of the grim facts: The Dow Jones Industrial Average was down a whopping 33.4 percent in 2008. Since October 2007, Americans have lost a mind-boggling $9 trillion in wealth from their retirement accounts, investments, and home values.

- More than 6 million Americans have lost their jobs since the recession began in late 2007, the most since World War II. As of November 2009 the unemployment rate had hit 10.2 percent. Nearly 16 million Americans were out of work.
- Home foreclosures soared by more than 81 percent in 2008. According to RealtyTrac, approximately 3.4 million families' homes will go into foreclosure by the end of 2009 compared with 2 million in 2007.
- Our national debt as of November 2009 was $12 trillion. That number has grown by $3.87 billion since September 2007. According to the Institute for Truth in Accounting, every citizen's share translates to nearly $235,000. The national deficit, which is the amount that the national debt grows each year, reached a record $1.4 trillion by October 2009. Hard to imagine that just eight years earlier, our nation actually had a surplus!

My goal here isn't to depress you but to suggest that there couldn't be a better time to take control of our financial lives. This crisis is complex and has many points of origin but one thing really resonates for me when I look at all the bleak statistics: We are a nation that spends more money than we take in. As individuals, Americans are among the world's worst savers and most in debt. In other words, many of us have simply abandoned personal financial discipline and paid a painful price for doing so.

Many people without any higher education have amassed large amounts of money by working hard and spending less money than they make. And I know people who have had every advantage, but spend more money than they make, and they will never be secure. In my work as an estate attorney, I've discovered the philosophy that most wealthy people understand and live by, no matter what their level of education—that it's not what you make, it's what you spend that counts most.

Maybe the most alarming trend that I've seen lately, and another reason that Wealth Watchers is so timely, is that so many people I've met are worried about how bad their children are with money. As I said, older parents would never have taught their children anything about the risks of using credit cards, or taking on mortgages that are unaffordable. When they were younger, there was no easy access to credit and people had to actually qualify for a home loan. And the amount of money they could borrow was limited. This generation paid cash for almost everything but their homes, and they took pride in paying off those home mortgages.

They couldn't have known that banks would one day entice people with easy credit, in much the same way that the tobacco industry made smoking so attractive. Now that credit card debt is skyrocketing and foreclosure rates and bankruptcies are breaking all kinds of records, we're becoming painfully aware of the lapse in educating our children about the risks of borrowing. And the time has come to say *enough*.

The massive personal debt in our country isn't just ruining the security of millions of families, it's obliterating our values. And when you think of us as a national "family," we aren't doing any better. The average family, like our government, now spends more than it takes in. The economic meltdown of the last few years was the direct result of this kind of myopic spending. Common sense tells us that we need to know how much money we can spend—and we need to spend less money than we have. Easier said than done—but it *can* be done. By embracing the Wealth Watchers philosophy that every day and every dollar make a difference, anyone can take that first step toward living smart. It may be overwhelming as is the first day of tackling any life-changing initiative, whether it's weight loss or giving up smoking. But there's something about the beginning of a journey that offers hope, and every journey begins with the first step.

Consumer spending is the fuel for our country's powerful economy and our material wealth has long been the envy of the world. But it seems as if the mantra of "spend, spend, spend"—even if it means maxing out multiple credit cards and living with mounting debt—has spawned a vast number of consumers who can't afford their purchases. They waste their lives juggling various forms of debt. Personal bankruptcies have soared since 2007 and when you add the subprime mortgage fiasco to the mix, it is not surprising that we're in the midst of a financial disaster.

As our new president has told us, there is no easy way out of the current mess, but I hope, by the time you read this, the economic picture will have taken a turn for the better. Economic trends historically move in cycles and great downturns are usually followed by periods of prosperity and stability. Nothing is guaranteed, but we need to learn over and over again that FDR was at least nearly right: *the only thing to fear is fear itself.*

But of course there *is* something else to fear, and that is *not learning* from our mistakes. Because regardless of the economic cycle we find ourselves in, we tend to ignore painful realities and slide back into the bad habits that got us into trouble in the first place. It's not as if there hasn't been a wave of personal finance advice over the past few decades. The magazines, websites, television and radio shows, and books are brimming with advice, but few seem to focus on the crucial issue of personal awareness and discipline. I've noticed, for example, that personal finance books tend to make many assumptions that aren't necessarily correct:

- Smart people invest in the stock market because over the long term it always goes up.
- A few well-made decisions about investments and savings at the outset, followed by occasional reviews, makes wealth-building automatic.
- When times get tough, you must simply cut back.

Those assumptions, of course, are based on the belief that most people, and the markets themselves, are financially stable. And nothing could be further from the truth. Though there has emerged in this country a growing group known as the mass affluent—people with enough socked away to be somewhere between comfortable and rich—most people are struggling to find a financial comfort zone in their lives. Many are a paycheck away from disaster and are neither investing in the stock market nor working with investment counselors on long-range plans that are within their realities. And regardless of where you stand financially, there's a good chance you or someone close to you struggles constantly with how much is reasonable to spend and how much debt is reasonable to carry.

Wealth Watchers was born from my own painful experience with money. Its foundation is a premise of simplicity and transparency: If we don't know how much we can spend without spending too much, we don't know when to stop. Multiple studies have shown that people spend more using credit cards than cash—anywhere from 12 percent to 40 percent more depending on which studies you read. A credit card puts a psychological distance between you and your money. The idea that you'll pay the bill later removes the "feel" of money leaving your possession the way that paying cash does.

Let me be clear here. I am not against credit cards or other credit products. In today's digital world, where more people shop online than in retail stores, credit products are indispensable. They are invaluable tools for managing our money if, and this is the big if, we are smart enough and careful enough to avoid making bad mistakes. Running up debt, paying astronomical interest rates, piling up expensive penalties, adding costly fees all make careless consumers their own worst enemies.

I don't have to tell you how toxic money troubles can be. Financial difficulty is the leading cause of divorce. If it is a challenge for one person to keep track of his or her spending, multiply that challenge by two people who must work from a shared and finite pot of money. If they aren't sharing information, there are bound to be meltdowns. Aside from poor health, there is nothing like bad finances to turn your world upside down. I have been there and it is not a place I care to visit again.

The Wealth Watchers principles are designed to empower people to get organized, increase their understanding of their income, expenses, and daily spending habits, help them create and maintain a budget, review their overall financial picture, set their financial goals, and in the end, reach one simple but essential calculation: daily disposable income (DDI). If you track your income and spending on a daily basis, amazing things happen, not the least of which is that you gain a crystal clear vision of your true financial landscape.

As you may notice, Wealth Watchers has a similar name and philosophy to the Weight Watchers program. Indeed, Weight Watchers was my inspiration for the concept. A life-changing brain injury, which I will describe in Chapter 2, impaired my ability to handle my finances and led to unwanted weight gain. It is also not a coincidence that our overconsumption of food and reliance on credit have ballooned at a similar rate. I went to Weight Watchers to help me drop the extra pounds, and in one of those "lightbulb" moments I realized that the solution to both my weight and spending problems lay in the simple, daily discipline of keeping track.

I think of Wealth Watchers both as a daily personal discipline and as a global movement. Just as we have long recognized the need to fight obesity by promoting healthy diets in our society, we must make an effort to promote fiscal health as well.

As the statistics tell us, this is a daunting challenge. In 2005, the personal savings rate of Americans dipped near zero and has remained close to that ever since. The last time something like this happened was in the Great Depression. Back then, it took innovative legislation, government-funded works projects, and ultimately World War II to pull the country out of the financial disaster that had lasted more than a decade. I know there are people reading this who are shaking their heads saying that the personal savings rate is a misleading figure because it doesn't take into account what people have (or, had!) invested in their retirement accounts or in home equity. But I'd like to ask those people how they would cover their living expenses if they lost a job, or a spouse, or developed a serious medical condition. I bet they would be wishing they also had a plain, old-fashioned savings account instead of having to drain their retirement accounts or gut their home equity.

The financial crisis had a swift impact on the savings rate. By May 2009, the savings rate had risen to 4 percent and it is clear that Americans are now rethinking their behavior. It will be interesting to see whether this trend will continue or whether we'll start spending more and saving less again when the economy rebounds. I hope that this time we'll have learned from our past mistakes.

In our lives, we have seen shocking financial behavior—based on a toxic combination of greed, ignorance, and arrogance—create the subprime mortgage crisis that set off not just a national but a global recession. But even if we take all of the sludge out of the current financial crisis, when it comes right down to it, we have, each of us, forgotten how important it is to save money. I'll leave it to the politicians and economists to point fingers and assign blame for the lack of oversight over the financial services industry. For me, the takeaway is all about personal responsibility, which is the foundation of Wealth Watchers. All the advances in the financial services industry—credit cards, ATMs, debit cards, online payment systems, PayPal—have made the flow of money accessible, fast, and convenient. But these innovations have also created a thick wall between people's spending habits and their awareness of what they can actually afford to spend. Listen to your car radio and you will inevitably hear an ad for consolidating credit card debt. Rampant credit card debt is like the obesity epidemic; we see the problem, we push for solutions, but we feel like we are taking one step forward and two steps back.

> How we choose to spend our time and money
> is very telling. Writing down everything you spend
> will be a reality check for your values.
> Also, you know you're doing well when you make
> a sacrifice and you feel smart—not deprived.

The Wealth Watchers philosophy is about helping individuals set and track a daily goal for spending and saving. My mission, with both the concept and this book, is to help people develop lifelong habits that embrace our core philosophy: "Every day and every dollar make a difference."

As I said, this current economic crisis can be a loud wake-up call for all of us. Winston Churchill once said, "The pessimist sees difficulty in every opportunity. The optimist sees the opportunity in every difficulty."

Despite our current economic hardships, I see unlimited opportunity for those who are willing to embrace the daily task of discipline and insight in their spending. Each day can make a tremendous difference—and the cumulative impact of the 365 days in a year can transform a life! What makes Wealth Watchers work is that it will help you seize each day, not waiting until the end of the month or the end of the quarter or the end of the year to change your life. I can't guarantee you'll find the kwan, but I can assure you'll find the path to the kwan if you arm yourself for the daily journey.

CHAPTER TWO

A Long Flight Home

The story of Wealth Watchers really begins on March 28, 2000 when my life changed, suddenly and unexpectedly, forever.

That afternoon, I boarded a plane near Steamboat Springs, Colorado with my close friend Mary Kay Clinton and her five-year-old daughter Katy Rose. After a wonderful ski vacation, we were heading home to Chicago and the last gray remnants of winter. We boarded the airplane directly from the tarmac, and I was such a tourist that I was snapping photos of us waiting to climb the stairs onto the plane.

The plane was not very full and since our assigned seats were in a cramped row, we moved to the emergency row and settled in. It didn't occur to us that Katy Rose was too young to be in an emergency row seat and the flight attendants didn't ask us to move. In the window seat, I almost immediately dozed off. Though the vacation was fun, I hadn't slept well and I nodded off quickly. As the plane ascended into clear skies, the oxygen masks suddenly dropped from above. The other passengers seemed startled but not truly alarmed. Groggy from sleep, I assumed it was a mistake, a malfunction. There was no announcement from the pilot or the flight attendants about a problem.

But when, seconds later, people started putting on their masks I began to worry. Our masks seemed stuck in the overheads. I began pulling at my mask with so much force that I was afraid I'd disconnect it from the oxygen supply. Mary Kay finally wrestled the masks down and we put ours on before helping Katy Rose with hers.

Within minutes, Mary Kay decided her mask wasn't functioning properly. Assuming that ours were fine, she got up to move across the aisle. The flight attendants appeared wearing masks and oxygen tanks. Now we knew something was wrong and I felt my first wave of real panic. The flight attendants wouldn't allow Katy Rose to stay in the emergency row so they moved her and her mother to another row. The flight attendant asked me if I could operate the emergency door. I nodded, but I hoped it wouldn't come to that.

The more time passed, the more I thought there was a good chance that we were all going to die. For some strange reason, I wanted to be sure that my IDs would be with my body so I wrapped the straps of my purse around one hand and held on tightly. As an estate planning lawyer, I'm probably a little morbid . . . maybe because we're always helping people prepare for the worst. I always encourage our clients to put letters for their children with their estate planning papers just in case something happens to them sooner rather than later. I thought about the letters I'd written to Eddie and Andy, my two boys from my first marriage. The letters were in a folder with my estate planning documents and were to be given to the boys in case I died unexpectedly while they were young. KC, my one-year-old daughter from my second marriage, was home with my husband Dan. I remember feeling awful that I'd not gotten around to writing a letter to her. Right before my thoughts grew muddled, I mused that it would be my only regret.

I felt as though someone's hand was covering my nose and mouth. Breathing was labored but, having never used an oxygen mask before, I made the foolish assumption that this was how they were supposed to work. I still hadn't heard any announcement from the pilot. Having no information was awful. Steamboat Springs sits high in the Rockies and the plane managed to clear the mountains and then leveled off and descended toward Denver for an emergency landing. At some point after we were at a lower altitude, the pilot announced that we could remove our oxygen masks. It was a huge relief to be able to breathe normally. I think I would have passed out if I'd had to wear the oxygen mask for another second.

We had a smooth landing in Denver. We had been airborne for only about thirty minutes. But I'm sure everyone on the plane had thought we were going to die. With no explanation, the airline personnel rushed us onto another flight to Chicago.

I asked the flight attendant from the new crew if there were free drinks for the people from the aborted flight. The guy sitting next to me looked concerned. "I think you're in shock," he said. I didn't pay much attention to his diagnosis, but it was true that something inside my head didn't feel right. When we landed in Chicago I found my mom, who had come to pick me up. I don't have much of a memory of the ride home except that my mother said, "I think something is wrong with you."

I told her I was fine and when I got in the door, I was just grateful to be home and safe with my family. But when I kissed Dan, I realized my face was numb. I thought it was funny—probably a good indication that my ability to think logically and clearly was impaired. I threw up in the shower, the wave of nausea coming suddenly with no warning. I knew our doctor, Jim Collins, was out on spring break since he and his family had been on my outbound flight from Chicago to Denver. He wouldn't be back for a few more days. I really didn't want to see anyone else, and I didn't want to go to the emergency room, so I did nothing.

The next morning, I felt a little off but I was able to go for a walk with Dan and KC. Outside in the brisk late winter air, I felt hot then cold then hot and then cold again. I had to keep sitting down along the way. We live just off the Riverwalk that winds through downtown Naperville and the brick pavers made me dizzy. I felt like I was going to pass out. By the time we made it to the playground at the other end of the Riverwalk Dan was alarmed. As a coach, he'd seen head trauma, and he thought I might have a concussion.

When I was finally examined a few days later, my doctor noticed that there was bleeding in my ear and he mentioned something about barotraumas, a type of injury due to dramatic changes in pressure that is common among scuba divers. He said that I'd probably be fine in a few days. But a few days came and went and I seemed to be even worse. He sent me to a neurologist who thought I might be suffering from migraines from the flight. It seemed an odd thing to say because I don't remember complaining of a headache.

It turned out that Mary Kay was dealing with some residual effects as well. She was feeling sick and wasn't doing very well. Mary Kay is a pit bull, and she was really annoyed that the airline hadn't acknowledged that there had been a problem on our flight. When she called the airline she was told that she was the only one on the flight who had complained. Not put off by that runaround, Mary Kay called the Federal Aviation Administration and demanded that they test the plane we had flown on. Amazingly, they did. They told me later that they had tested the plane and found that the masks in our row had malfunctioned again during the test.

That didn't do me much good. I was just struggling to get through the day and not thinking clearly enough to worry about culpability. I just wanted to feel like my old self.

Friends suggested I should get some rest and that I'd be fine. But I wasn't fine. I was an absolute mess. My sons, who were eleven and sixteen at the time, had come home from a spring break with their father a few days after I made it home. I didn't want to tell them what had happened to me because I didn't want them to be afraid to fly. But it was obvious. I couldn't even say their names correctly. I couldn't understand what they were saying when they were both talking at the same time. They were so frustrated with me that I had to tell them about the flight. "You're just going to have to cut me some slack for a while," I told them and they both started to cry.

Eddie disappeared and came back a few minutes later to tell me that the airline was on the phone for me. He had called the airline on his own and started yelling at people until he was put in touch with someone from the Claims Department. When I got on the phone I didn't know whether I should be embarrassed or proud. How funny that Mary Kay, a multiple Emmy Award–winning television producer, had had a terrible time getting anyone to take her call . . . and my sixteen-year-old son was able to get through to the right people on his first try. The airline representative seemed genuinely concerned about what had happened to me and he promised to have someone from their medical team follow up with me. But nobody ever did.

I figured the airline's reaction was standard operating procedure. Deny liability. Nearly a year later, I filed a lawsuit which, at this writing more than nine years after the incident, is still pending. Fortunately for Mary Kay, she began to feel better quickly and had no residual aftereffects. In my addled state of mind, I didn't put two and two together: She'd found a functioning oxygen mask quickly enough to avoid injuring her brain. By staying in my seat, I had sealed my fate.

After I had an EEG, the neurologist's nurse called to let me know that the test showed slowing, a definite sign of a brain injury. Even though I had begun to suspect as much, I was stunned. It was so devastating because in my heart of hearts I was hoping that nothing was wrong and that I would be back to normal any day. In fact, four more months went by before I had a clear moment. Life became a series of muddled days and nights during which I tried fruitlessly to recover. At least I'd finally gotten an accurate diagnosis. My doctor said it was an anoxic brain injury—damage caused by a lack of oxygen to the brain. When the brain doesn't receive proper amounts of glucose and oxygen, nerves in the cortex where brain cells originate are damaged. It takes only five minutes for a lack of oxygen to permanently damage the brain. I'd had that mask on for nearly twenty minutes. My brain had actually slowed down, the synapses weren't connecting correctly. I was staggered. Here I was just forty years old and I had brain damage. How serious it was, how permanent it was, I didn't know. But it was very real and very scary.

It is hard to describe how strange it was to lose control of my life in this way. Outwardly, I looked fine and normal so everyone expected me to be able to do everything I had done before. I hated having to explain what was going on. I sometimes felt like drawing a huge scar on my forehead. During those first few months, I had so many car accidents, mostly backing into our own cars in our driveway. Sometimes, when I couldn't remember where I was driving, I'd just have to pull over, take a deep breath, and try really hard to stay calm and think. One of my worst memories is of forgetting to pick Eddie up from a golf course. By the time I remembered and drove to the golf course, it was dark and there wasn't a single car in the parking lot. I found Eddie sitting on a curb all by himself. I hugged him and cried and told him I would never forget him again. It wasn't the end of the world for Eddie. He was finally going to get the cell phone that he'd been asking for.

I tried to go to work but it became increasingly difficult to concentrate, to remember what I knew, or to interact with clients. I couldn't sit at the computer without getting dizzy, and I simply could not focus on what was on the screen. I watched my livelihood go up in smoke.

My injury put serious strain on my marriage as well. Dan has the patience of a saint but I was driving him crazy. I think it must be true that when you're not well, you take it out on the person closest to you. Poor Dan. He bore the brunt of everything that had been upended by my brain injury. He had to get used to me being fatigued, forgetful, and crabby. I don't really remember this, but he said the greatest change in me was that I was always mad at him. Things got so bad that we wound up in marriage counseling. Dan is a very private person, but he was so desperate for help that he told the marriage counselor that my poor memory was driving him crazy. This was a turning point in my recovery. I realized that I could no longer convince myself that I was always right. I was going to have to start relying on the people around me to help me get through this. But that would be easier said than done.

I've always been a determined, organized, and independent person. I'd never been overwhelmed by pressure, and I'd successfully started my own law firm, raised a family, and stayed fit. Now it was as though a curtain had come down on that life and I had entered some kind of Twilight Zone. I can remember lying in bed at night wondering "Why me? How could this have happened to me? Nothing bad ever happens to me." I had always been able to make the best of any bad situation, but I was pretty sure I'd never be able to say that anything good came out of my brain injury.

I couldn't even do the everyday things, like pay bills and oversee the family's finances, chores that I'd always enjoyed doing. Brain injured people tend to be terrible with money. Unaware of how much they are spending, they forget to pay bills and lose track of their financial accounts. All this was suddenly happening to me but I was too stubborn to ask for help.

The first two years were the worst. I could barely function. KC was just a year old when this happened and one night, I put a plate of food in front of her as if she could feed herself. She wound up just dumping it on her head. I thought it was hysterical, but Dan was worried. I couldn't work at anywhere near my old pace and I would sometimes meet with clients and forget to ask them the right questions. Sometimes I didn't even recognize people I had just met with two weeks earlier. I began working with a neuropsychologist to help me manage my law practice. I made dozens of lists of everything I needed to do just to have some hope of keeping up. My law practice hung on by a slim thread as my ability to handle multiple tasks was disappearing I asked my brother George to help me pay our bills. Dan, who had always been very solid in handling his own finances before we were married, had been trying to help me with our finances, but for some strange reason I ignored him. Maybe it's because I didn't want him to know how bad things really were. For the first time in my life, money became a real challenge. My income tanked and my spending shot through the roof. I once lost my sunglasses—just one of many things I lost during this crisis—and when I went to buy a new pair, I couldn't decide which ones I liked. So I bought them all! That was just not something the old me would ever do. Now, all bets were off.

I told Dan that we were carrying a balance on our credit cards, something we'd rarely done before, and he suggested that, horror of horrors, maybe we needed to go on a budget. I told

> ## "Be Prepared."
> *Motto of the Boy Scouts of America*
>
> Something will always go wrong, especially if you're not ready for it. Talk to your banker about automatically transferring a certain amount of money each month into a savings account that can be your safety net.

him that everything would be fine. I was sure I'd be back to my old income before we knew it. But I was wrong. A big blow came when we received a credit card bill from a company I didn't recognize with a $20,000 balance on it. I had enough sense to call the credit card company to ask about it, assuming it was a mistake. They told me that I'd received one of those promotional deals in which they include what looks like a legitimate check for some product or service. Most people toss those away but apparently I had signed the check and deposited it in our bank account as if we'd suddenly been given a surprise gift of twenty grand. I went back to our bank statement for the month and sure enough, I had deposited the check with absolutely no memory of doing so.

I did finally have the presence of mind to call our accountant, Tom Weber, and ask him for help. I had no idea what was going wrong. I asked him what seemed like an odd question: "How much money can I spend?" And his answer was brilliant: "Alice, you can't spend more money than you make." I think he meant to say that you *shouldn't* spend more money than you make because of course you can and I had. Big time. But it was a loud wake-up call. How much money did we make, and how much money could we spend? I became determined to find that magic number.

It was a battle, let me tell you. As things spiraled out of control, I started wishing that someone would tell me I was terminally ill. I didn't want to live the rest of my life like this. I would rather have died. Actually, money had nothing to do with my death wish. I felt wretched, trapped in a perpetual fog. And if that wasn't enough, out of nowhere I started gaining weight.

Fortunately, I come from a large family and their support brought back my optimism that I could get through this. My mom, in particular, was a lifesaver. When I had reached the end of my rope and felt like I couldn't be a lawyer anymore, she encouraged me to take time off from work and lent me enough money to keep our office up and running without me. That month off was exactly what I needed, a chance to shut off my brain and begin to heal. I began to feel better after that and I signed up for Weight Watchers in order to shed the weight I'd gained. Weight Watchers turned out to be one of the best things that ever happened to me. Everyone has heard the name Weight Watchers, but some may be unaware of its philosophy, which is what makes it the most brilliant weight loss program available.

Simply put, Weight Watchers is not about dieting. Weight Watchers believes a healthy body results from a healthy lifestyle, which means mental, physical, and emotional health. Best of all, it's not dependent on prepackaged foods. They encourage you to set and track a daily goal for what you eat and part of that includes eating foods from the right food groups. They never tell you that you can't eat anything. In fact, they would say that you can eat anything you want as long as you plan for it. The goal at Weight Watchers is to help people make healthy eating decisions. They stress the value of exercise, good food choices in the right portions, and most of all, the importance of keeping track of what you are doing everyday so you will know exactly how many calories you are taking in. It's not about dieting, it's about *changing behavior and making good choices.* It was the perfect place for me. The original Weight Watchers plan was based on people attending meetings where they not only get valuable information but invaluable support and encouragement, and this is what they offered me.

At one of these meetings in 2002, it just hit me. The same principles that applied to weight loss could also work with money. It meant keeping track of money in the same way we kept track of our food intake "points." It also meant understanding down to each day how much you could spend without going into debt. Every single day would be important. It was more than keeping a budget; it was about changing your *financial* behavior.

When I used these methods for my own financial issues I made remarkable progress. I started to share the idea and its promise with others and it struck a chord. In fact, it was downright contagious! Like Weight Watchers, it was a simple system of accounting and accountability . . . in fact, the system *is* the solution—simple, no excuses.

The name Wealth Watchers came to me in my sleep—when I do some of my best thinking—and a new business was born, which in my diminished state was probably the last thing I needed. If you are wondering how I could have even considered starting a business in the midst of this life crisis, you ask a reasonable question. The truth is, at the outset, I didn't envision starting my own business. I thought, if this concept could work for me, wouldn't there be a great opportunity to create a business and sell it to some ambitious entrepreneur? But as I pushed my way forward, I began to see that the concept was not only working for me, but that I might just be able to make this work on a larger scale if I had enough strong support, good advice, and very good luck. I never thought anything good would come out of the brain injury. But having something exciting and new to work for proved to be a potent medicine for my soul, and I began to think that maybe I had been through my ordeal for a reason.

Before my brain injury, managing money was effortless for me. I rarely made mistakes. When I was younger and money was tight, I kept a strict budget. As I grew successful and made more money, I discarded the budget. I no longer had to worry about having enough set aside to the pay the bills so I spent wisely but freely and didn't give money a second thought. Arrogance put an end to the financial discipline I'd relied on when things weren't so easy.

For many of us, the American dream is about reaching that point of financial security and freedom where you can buy a nice home, support your family comfortably, buy a decent car, take a special vacation, and afford to send your kids to college. When you are doing OK financially, you don't need to sit down every night to log in every single dime you spent that day.

But life can change very suddenly. Getting complacent about money is the surest way to get into trouble. I have learned the hard way that we set ourselves up for bad luck when we forget to be prepared for the worst. And, as many of us parents know, making things look too easy is a poor lesson for our children.

Wealth Watchers is really nothing more than a means to a positive end. It is the voice on your shoulder reminding you to think before you spend. As you will see, the discipline of keeping careful track of your spending needn't be a burden. In fact it can guarantee a completely fresh way to think about your financial condition.

My own long struggle with the brain injury and its impact on my financial life made Wealth Watchers far more than a business opportunity for me. It became a discipline, my lifeline to financial awareness. The first year we kept our daily Wealth Watchers journal, Dan and I spent $12,000 less than we had spent the year before. Looking at my financial mistakes after the brain injury, I honestly think we would have been bankrupt if we had not used Wealth Watchers. For example, I had always made savvy real estate decisions. I bought my own home when I was a single mother and watched it appreciate in value. We invested in a few condos that also appreciated dramatically. But just before the real estate bubble burst, I convinced Dan that we should cash out of the equity in our home since builders were offering ridiculous amounts of money to tear down homes in our neighborhood. We found a perfect home to move to that was only four blocks away and closed the deal on the new house before we sold our old home. And then it happened: the collapse of the subprime mortgage market and the beginning of the slide into the worst economy we have faced during my lifetime. And there we were, paying two mortgages when we could barely afford one. We had a fifteen-year mortgage on the first house that would have been paid off if it weren't for my lost income. We had to refinance it into a thirty-year mortgage. Besides funding two mortgages, we have also carried the costs of college, the costs of a law firm, and the costs of a start-up business all with lines of credit and home equity loans. I didn't realize how bad things were, mostly because I am such an optimist and I always believed things would work out. But I've had to ask for help from my family to get me through more than a few tough moments.

And I shudder to think how difficult it would have been to pass along some financial awareness to our kids without Wealth Watchers as a template.

It's easy to talk about people's struggles with money but if you are financially secure and have never worried about missing a bill payment, you can really never understand the agony of living on the edge of financial disaster. The *New York Times,* on February 7, 2009, ran an insightful article about "Plan B," that "whimsical reverie about the life that you could swap for the one that you were leading." Plan B used to be that bed-and-breakfast you'd run in Vermont or the round-the-world trip you'd take after you retired. Now, it has become the dreadful reality of a once secure life gone awry. "The old Plan B was a lark that you could enjoy even if you never got past the dreaming phase," the article said. "The new Plan B is a menace you can fear even if you're fully employed. It's a threat rather than an option."

So many of us have unwittingly stumbled into the new Plan B. Living off home equity loans and credit cards, facing the loss of a home, spending most of a retirement account, standing a short step away from financial hardship or disaster are unfortunate facts of life without a safety net.

My brain injury has pushed me into my own Plan B. As my ability to work diminished and my decision making became more and more muddled, my financial choices wreaked havoc. And though I'm resigned to the struggle that the brain injury has caused, I am determined to keep working and not to give up.

The concept of Wealth Watchers came to me in 2002 but it took me years to gather the courage to actually start it up. On one level, it was unthinkable to start a new business. It was hard enough to keep up with my estate planning practice. And for some unfounded reason, I worried that Wealth Watchers would hurt my reputation as a lawyer. But by the end of 2005, I had enough encouragement from people I trusted that I decided to go for it. After all, Ray Kroc didn't start McDonald's until he was fifty-two, and he ran it on borrowed money for a long time. I figured if Mr. Kroc thought it was a good idea to borrow money to start a business, then it was. Over the past three years, the concept has been validated not only by friends, family, and individuals who have adopted the Wealth Watchers program, but by a growing list of schools and companies that have incorporated Wealth Watchers as a foundation for promoting financial literacy.

So let me introduce you to the concept. As you will find in Part II of this book, I've provided all the Wealth Watchers tools you will need to get started. The only ingredients you have to provide are the will and the discipline to change your life.

CHAPTER THREE

Getting Started, Getting Organized

My mother has an unusual philosophy about what makes her feel financially secure. All she really needs, she tells me, is a full tank of gas and a roll of stamps. If I could get her to use email more, she could probably eliminate half her expenses. But for most of us, my mom's Thoreau-like simplicity, though enviable, is just not going to cut it.

I think it's fair to say that somewhere along the road to the American Dream, the wheels came off for a vast number of people. Though there is a long list of economic factors that are out of our personal control—global recessions, for example—if we are honest with ourselves, we would quote the beloved cartoon character Pogo, who said, "We have met the enemy and he is us."

When it comes to financial stability, we as a society have gotten ourselves into countless financial messes. As a nation, we have that $11 trillion national debt that I mentioned earlier. You can't blame yourself for that one. But how about this: Consumer debt stands at $2.56 trillion, up 22 percent since 2000, and the average household credit card balance is nearly $8,600, up 15 percent since 2000. Credit card fees have skyrocketed as credit card debt has soared. And a lot of us feel like we are drowning in that debt.

Having my brain injury gave me a front-row seat on this financial roller coaster. I've gotten a strong appreciation for what it is like to be overwhelmed by financial problems. It is not something you grow to accept and the discomfort and stress never completely disappear.

What we could all use—adults and young people alike—is a major dose of financial education, and trust me, I'll get up on my soapbox about the need for a widespread financial literacy effort in this country throughout this book. It just kills me that so many of our children get absolutely no financial guidance from their parents or the schools. I'm hoping that what you learn here in Wealth Watchers, you will share with your kids—or better yet, give them the book to read as well.

Wealth Watchers is not a complex program. But there are some basic questions you need to consider. Here is the most important one: *How much money do you really have available to spend?*

If I were to ask you how much money you can spend every day, what would that number be? My guess is that you have no idea. Most people don't. But there actually is a number . . . you just have to figure it out. That is what Wealth Watchers will help you do. You may think it's silly to have a daily number, but it's a great way to have your very own daily reality check about where you stand with your spending and saving. You will probably be very surprised by what you discover. Because if you think about it, how we choose to spend our money is very telling.

Given the incredible impact money has on our lives, it is amazing to me that so few people have any idea how much they can spend before running into trouble. Would any coach go into the Super Bowl without a game plan? When we careen through our daily lives, tossing credit cards on checkout counters or pulling cash out of our wallets for random purchases or lunch with a friend, we are flying blind. It's not surprising that so many people spend more than they should. Our emotional and intellectual trigger for spending is based on the idea that we'll worry about keeping score at the end . . . the end of the month, the end of the quarter, the end of the year. We assume, hope, pray that there will always be enough to cover our costs. When there isn't, we shrug, feel a twinge of remorse, and then start the same pattern over again. The heart wants what the heart wants, right? And if the heart wants that $4 cup of coffee or that $15 martini, what's wrong with that?

Does anyone really care if they waste $4? Does anyone even care if they waste $15? But I'm pretty sure that all of us would care if we lost $1,460 ($4 x 365); or $5,475 ($15 x 365). Because those are the types of expenses that we can so mindlessly take on every single day of the year. The ideals behind Wealth Watchers are intended to serve as an eye-opener. (And let me be clear that I love Starbucks and I'm not singling out specialty coffee drinks above any other daily expense you might want to reconsider. But it is not a coincidence that Starbucks has closed hundreds of stores and faced a serious decline during the recession. Apparently, quite a few people decided that $4 lattes were no longer affordable. The company recognized its customers' growing financial dilemma and started offering cheaper "instant" Starbucks coffee, for under a dollar a cup, as one way to address the financial crisis.)

And it's not at all far-fetched that someone casually spends $4 a day on something they don't really need. And the $15 martini? Hmmm . . . maybe a good strong drink is what we really need to try to forget about what's going wrong in our world. But as I noted, a $15 a day expense will still cost you $5,475 a year! So you don't have a martini every day? Neither do I, but I would not be at all surprised if there is another way that we might spend $15 in a day without thinking twice about it. A lunch with colleagues, a stop at a clothing store, a session on iTunes can easily cost that much. Personally, I'd rather have the money in the bank. Maybe that's not true for everyone, of course. And if you add up those kinds of expenditures that you make all the time, you will get an idea of what Wealth Watchers is about. The concept is built upon setting a daily goal, keeping track of daily spending, and reaching your overall spending and saving goal.

Why does anyone do anything if it's not to reach a goal? And when it comes to money, why is it that so many of us avoid setting a goal? Are we too busy to even consider it? Do we assume we are too young to have to worry about it? Are we too overwhelmed by life's pressures to be thinking about it? Well, today there is no excuse. If you can't think of a financial goal by the end of this chapter then I'll set one for you: *Happiness.*

Most people believe in the old adage that money can't buy happiness. That may be true but there's evidence to the contrary. The *New York Times*, in April 2008, reported on a new study by two Brookings Institution researchers that showed that income does indeed matter. A recent Gallup poll revealed that in the United States, about 90 percent of people in households making at least $250,000 a year called themselves "very happy." In households with income below $30,000, only 42 percent of people gave the same answer.

For me, this validates the Wealth Watchers concept. The more money you have to spend, the less you have to worry about paying the bills and stressing out over every penny. But there is more to it than that. A big paycheck isn't necessarily the catalyst for contentment. The real source of happiness is having control over your money and knowing that you have more coming in than going out.

Jean Chatzky, one of my favorite financial authors, wrote a

book called *The Ten Commandments of Financial Happiness*. Chatzky set out to find the common traits among people who are happy about where they stand with money. And the results are surprising. At the end of the day, the happiness ratio had very little to do with the *amount* of income. It actually had everything to do with the fact that people *knew where they stood* when it came to money. They had a good handle on all of their bills, and they had a plan for what they would do with their money.

WHERE TO BEGIN?

For most people, the most difficult part of the journey to financial awareness is facing the task of getting organized. You won't be able to use Wealth Watchers effectively if you don't stay on top of the flow of bills and other financial information that impact your life. I can empathize with anyone who thinks it's just too depressing to focus on money like that, but burying your head in the sand is only going to make things worse. I've been told by several credit counselors that people come into their office with grocery bags full of unopened bills. Thank goodness these people are reaching out for help. There is a light at the end of the tunnel. But you can't expect to get to the end of the tunnel if you don't do anything to move in the right direction.

There are so many variations on organizational techniques. I don't know that there's one that's better than another. But you at least have to have a system. Any system is better than none. I know this is easier said than done, but if you pay your bills as they come in, you won't ever have to worry about being late. I know that many of us need to wait until the next paycheck arrives before paying our bills. But wouldn't it feel great if we could get ahead of our bills so they really could be paid on the day they were received? For any financial adviser out there who thinks that people would be missing out on the "float" of keeping their money in the bank for as long as possible, I'm here to tell you that you are doing a huge disservice to people who are trying to wrap their arms around something that may seem simple to you—floating money for a few weeks would be of minimal benefit to most people. And any benefit would be wiped out by late fees if they don't get their bills paid on time. So if your personal banking center consists of stacks of papers—bills, bank statements, pay stubs, and such—scattered around the kitchen, the dining room, a desk in your den, a grocery bag, you must bite the bullet and dive in to make sense of this mess.

GETTING ORGANIZED

Step One on your road to becoming a Wealth Watcher is to set aside one place where all of your bills, bank statements, and other financial information will be stored. A file cabinet, a desk drawer, a big cardboard box—as long as it becomes the center of your financial universe, it will suffice.

By getting a firm understanding of your income and your expenses, you will be able to figure out how much money you really have to spend. Check out several of your past bank statements and credit card statements to get a feel for where your money has been going as opposed to where your money should be going. Find out exactly what it costs you to live each month. Then go through your pay stubs or other sources of income for the past few months to find out what your net income is each month. Just how much is left after all of the withholdings for taxes, insurance, and so on. Knowledge is power. This will be worth the effort. A **monthly budget** will help pull these numbers together.

CREATING A MONTHLY BUDGET

The Monthly Budget on pages 141–142 lists typical monthly expenses that someone might face. Everyone is different so you may need to create different categories to fit your particular expenses.

> **Monthly net income**—List all available income you receive each month.
>
> **Monthly fixed expenses**—List every expense that is the same each month (mortgage, car payment, child care).
>
> **Monthly semi-fixed expenses**—List every expense that you have each month that varies in amount, such as utilities. When listing both your fixed and semi-fixed expenses, ask yourself if any of these payments can be lowered.

Reviewing Your Financial Picture

Keep in mind that necessary expenses such as food, shelter, clothing, transportation, medical needs, education, or child care should have priority in your planning. Subtract your **total fixed** and **semi-fixed expenses** from your **total net income** to reach your monthly disposable income (MDI), otherwise known as spending money.

Determining Your Disposable Income

Disposable income is income available each month after paying your fixed and semi-fixed expenses. The Monthly Budget will provide the amount of your disposable income, which can be projected for the year. That number will be divided by 365 to give you a daily target that will be known as your **daily dispos-**

able income, or DDI. Keep in mind "The Power of 365." Any savings times 365 is a worthwhile goal. If your income changes each month, you just need to make a conservative estimate of what you think your net income will be each month.

SETTING YOUR GOAL

There's a saying, "If you don't know where you are going, you'll probably end up somewhere else." Reaching financial comfort is dependent on many things, but having a clear goal is the most important step. Setting specific long- and short-term goals—anything from fulfilling your dream to travel abroad to something more practical like paying off your credit cards—is crucial. Having a specific set of goals will provide a constant incentive to financial responsibility.

What is more important to you:

- Saving for vacation, education, home ownership or retirement?
- Spending less money than you make?
- Knowing where your money goes?
- _____ (You fill in the blank)

The Bare Minimum

Share your goal

Tell someone you trust that you are on a mission to be better with money. Just telling another person is going to make you more likely to reach your goal. Even better, see if they are up for joining you. There's nothing like having an accountability partner to keep you on the right path.

Know your numbers

Pull together your past few banks statements or your past few months of bills. Find your daily number (DDI).

You can go through the budget calculation on page 4 of the Wealth Watchers Journal (page 142 of this book) to calculate down to the day how much money you can spend without going into debt. Question every monthly payment you have and try to find a less expensive alternative.

Over the course of a month, record every purchase you make in a journal, and the form of payment: whether it is cash, check, credit, or debit card. Get into the habit of writing down the amount you spend immediately after you spend it. There's something so manageable about taking on one day at a time. If you have to write down everything you spend at the time you are making a purchase, I guarantee you that you will have a "think before you spend" moment. Even if you make mistakes, you'll learn to make better decisions going forward.

JOURNALING

We all need a reality check. Recording your daily spending will help you track and understand where your money goes. It forces that "think before you spend" moment I just mentioned. Even John D. Rockefeller, Jr., one of the world's richest men, insisted that each of his six children keep a ledger and write down every single penny they spent. The only items that should be included in your journal are expenditures aside from fixed and semi-fixed expenses. These would include groceries, gasoline, car repairs, clothing, restaurants, medical expenses, and others that might be unique to you and your life. Remember that you can have almost anything you want as long as you plan ahead and save for

> The best education is by example.
> Writing down everything you spend shows that
> you're "choosing" to spend money. So many of us
> randomly pull out a credit card for everything and
> the message seems to be that spending is effortless.
> It's not. It's our choice to be smart or careless.

it. That's why expenses such as travel, luxury items, and gifts should be the target for better planning.

The reason we recommend a journal is that it's next to impossible to keep track of everything without one. Journaling also erases that voice we hear in the back of our minds that wonders "where did all of my money go?"

Let me share Stan's story with you. Stan was not the type of person I'd expected at Wealth Watchers. He is a twenty-year veteran at a leading technology firm, where he is a program manager in the IT group. He has an MBA from a highly regarded university and lives in an upscale suburb with his wife and teenage daughters. From all appearances, he is the picture of financial health and stability.

But when I met him, he told me he wanted more control over his finances. He had an extended work project in the Chicago area and while he was there, he read about Wealth Watchers. Stan's wife was attending Weight Watchers at the time and he had gone to some meetings with her. He was intrigued by the Wealth Watchers concept and came to one of our meetings.

"It is ironic that I received all As in accounting, I manage projects with multimillion-dollar budgets but I still struggle with my own finances," Stan said at our meeting. Sound familiar? How many of us are incredibly successful in so many parts of our lives but grapple with our finances?

Stan's biggest struggle was one of the most common that we see, out-of-control credit card debt. He wanted to rein in his credit card spending, not only because it had been steadily mounting over the years, but because his wife had left her job for family reasons and he needed tighter control over the family's finances. I can't tell you how many times I've heard versions of this story. As the recession continues, this kind of financial predicament has reached epidemic proportions in our country.

For Stan, the first step to regaining financial control was to start his Wealth Watchers journal. "I saw immediate benefits," he said. "It is important to try to write down an expense as soon as possible so you are forced to think about how you are spending your money. Writing down the expense before making a purchase is even better because it makes you think twice about the purchase. It also gets you to focus on how much money you spend on nonessential items."

The key for Stan is maintaining discipline. Unlike a fad diet that helps you lose weight quickly but offers no way to keep it off, journaling forces you to maintain discipline in personal finance. This is especially true, as Stan points out, when extra money comes in and you are tempted to indulge.

If, like Stan, you are struggling to get ahead financially, a journal is the essential tool. Journaling allows you to see ways to be smarter with your time and money. This daily exercise may even inspire you to go after a higher paying job. Whatever the situation, a journal will allow you to make better choices in your daily spending.

Even if you're independently wealthy, you probably dislike wasting money as much as someone who is on a tight budget. In general, people who amass great fortunes do so not only because they are business savvy but because they are careful about their spending and saving. If you're a business owner, you may want to use a Wealth Watchers program to set a good example for your employees or customers—as the folks are doing at McDonalds, Visa, and other financial institutions, organizations that have embraced the Wealth Watchers concept. There's nothing like seeing that the boss cares where an employee's time and money goes to encourage the responsible use of a business expense account. If you're a student, a journal may be the only way to save yourself an overdraft fee or keep yourself on track to get through school without accumulating massive debt. Students constantly make the mistake of believing that an ATM balance is an accurate picture of how much money they have to spend. As I said earlier, they forget that there might be a charge or check that hasn't cleared yet. That mistake is usually very costly and students can afford it less than anyone.

In *Poor Richard's Almanac,* published 250 years ago, Benjamin Franklin wrote: "Small leaks sink great ships." Such wisdom is as relevant today as it was then. When you start tracking where your money goes, you'll find those small leaks. If you can avoid small leaks you'll stay above water . . . and then some. Benjamin Franklin's wisdom, especially about money, is legendary. He also wrote in his famed *Almanac,* "Industry and frugality are the means of procuring wealth and thereby securing virtue." It's a little bit wordy but I think it could be a motto for Wealth Watchers.

Wealth Watchers also stresses the importance of a single day. The simple difference between drinking water with your lunch and drinking iced tea can be something like $3 when you consider the cost itself, the sales tax, and the tip that goes along with the order. We always bring out a calculator during our meetings just to emphasize the impact of simple, daily choices over a year. It's hard to believe that we could spend $1,095 in a year on something as insignificant as iced tea . . . but it's the truth. We make these mindless decisions every single day. Personally, I'd rather put that money toward our vacation fund, but my aim is not to lecture you on how to spend your money. One person's idea of waste may be another person's well considered choice.

If you're married, you may face different challenges in handling your money. I've met couples who keep all their money separate, right down to their checking accounts for paying bills. But experience tells me that most couples pool their income, savings, and share a joint checking account. If that is true for you, you should coordinate your journaling efforts with your partner or your effort will be wasted. My husband and I have kept separate journals and then compared them on Sundays so that we don't work at odds with each other. Here are some other methods that work for us and for other Wealth Watchers.

Daily Total—Add your daily expenditures and record the total amount for each day. Do not include fixed and semi-fixed expenditures. They have already been factored into the determination of your disposable income.

Weekly Total—Add your daily totals for the week and record that figure in the Weekly Summary box at the bottom of that week's journal. Include your partner's figures if applicable. Your average daily total will be the weekly total divided by seven.

Monthly Total—Add your daily totals for the month and record the figure on the respective Monthly Budget Summary located in the back of the journal in this book. The average daily total

will be the monthly total divided by the number of days in that month.

Quarterly Total—Add your monthly totals for the quarter and record that figure on the respective Quarterly Budget Summary located at the back of this journal. The average daily total will be the quarterly total divided by the number of days in that quarter.

How Well Did You Do?

The difference between your DDI goal and your actual average daily total of expenses will show you if you are staying on track. Were you over or under your targeted daily disposable income? A plus (+) sign next to your number would indicate that you had a savings of that much per day. A minus (-) sign next to your number would indicate that you overspent by that much per day. *Any savings times 365 will be a worthwhile goal.*

Trust me, half the battle in managing your finances is staying organized. I have gotten such great feedback from Wealth Watchers members about this part of the program that I am certain it can help you. Our lives are so demanding—from jobs to family to school to health care—that it is no surprise that people lose track of their financial status. It is very satisfying to corral and vanquish that feeling of being a day late and a dollar short. I'll offer some details on some of the financial topics we wrestle with in our lives in the next chapter.

CHAPTER FOUR

The Details

When we are overwhelmed by our finances, many of us shove bills into a desk drawer and hope they'll miraculously disappear. But ignoring real financial problems will only compound misery. A young friend once confided in me that he was having a terrible time keeping up with his bills. He told me it had become so depressing that he no longer opened his mail or took phone calls from strangers. And that he'd been too embarrassed to talk to anyone about what was going on.

My young friend had turned a full 180 degrees away from the Wealth Watchers philosophy. In the vain hope that his troubles would vanish, he had abandoned control of his money. I suggested that he open his mail, make a list of all the bills, and write down everything he owed. The total amounted to less than $3,000, not so bad, after all. By facing the truth of his situation, he had caught the problem before it spiraled completely out of control.

After my brain injury, I put on enough extra weight that my clothes no longer fit. (I can't believe I did this, but I gave away my thin clothes so I had to buy new clothes when I lost the weight. Ugh! Just what I needed, more expenses!) I had gained twenty pounds and managed to lose nearly nine pounds on my own, but because I couldn't get rid of those last eleven pounds I joined Weight Watchers. I faithfully followed the program and once I had reached my goal weight, the leader of our group

asked me to stand up in front of the other members to be acknowledged. I was extremely embarrassed doing this because there were people in the group who had lost 100 pounds or more. My measly eleven pounds seemed to pale in comparison, but I was given the same recognition. In fact the group leader said "Wouldn't it be nice if we were all smart enough to get help when we were only eleven pounds overweight?"

The same is true with our finances: Wouldn't people be far better off getting help when they first encountered a problem rather than waiting for it to turn into a catastrophe?

Not surprisingly, there is a clear relationship between the rise in consumer debt (and the decline in our personal savings rate) and the rise in obesity. Of course, most of us could make better choices when it comes to food and money. But for me, there's more to it. The wave of "innovations" in the financial services industry over the past two decades was accompanied by a similar wave of new "convenient" products introduced by the food industry.

The financial services industry provided new products that offered quick and easy access to credit and so the increased opportunity to overspend. Similarly, the food industry introduced an array of prepared foods that may have made meal time easier, but—with their increased calories and unhealthy ingredients—also spurred consumers to overeat. Just as getting back to basics in banking makes good sense, so does eating healthier, unprocessed foods.

In any case, ignoring or hiding from your financial problems, as my young friend tried to do, is not the answer. Gail Cunningham, a spokesperson for the National Foundation for Credit Counseling, told the *New York Times* a similar tale. She said that people must first admit they have a problem, as they would in a twelve-step program, in order to begin fixing it. She said many people come to the NFCC offices every day with shopping bags filled with unopened bills. I know someone who lost his health insurance simply because he couldn't bring himself to open his mail. After undergoing an expensive medical test, he found that he wasn't insured because he had missed the payment for his health insurance premium. To make matters worse, he was diagnosed with a condition that makes him uninsurable, so that he has to rely on the high-risk health insurance program offered through the State of Illinois—though even this is too expensive.

Dan and I have discovered that the Wealth Watchers system has helped us get smarter about our monthly bills. Instead of blindly paying our bills each month, I decided to tackle them one at a time. I created a family budget that is built according to scale, from the largest to the smallest expenses, and then went through each category to see where we might be able to cut costs. I've divided the list into **fixed expenses, semi-fixed expenses** (housing, insurance, transportation, child care, college), and **discretionary expenses,** which I'll discuss in Chapter 5. You might wonder why food is not on the fixed expense list. While it's clearly an essential expense, how you shop, what you buy, how much you spend is purely discretionary. In fact, it is the same with clothing and safeguarding your home. You may choose to make your own version of the list, and that is fine. The goal is to know what you've spent and how much you have to spend.

So here goes:

FIXED EXPENSES

Depending on your age, your family size, your lifestyle, your geography, your health, and your occupation, fixed expenses vary. But taking a monthly chore and turning it into a relatively painless ritual is the foundation of the Wealth Watchers program. Within this exercise, you can address both immediate financial issues and bigger issues that will have an impact on your future. When you are paying the rent or the mortgage, for example, you should think about which option is the right one for you and your family at this particular point in your lives.

Housing

A decade of home buying that resulted in the subprime mortgage crisis has revived the debate over the virtues of owning versus renting. With increased opportunities for easy mortgages, the number of homeowners ballooned in the past two decades, growing significantly in proportion to renters. During this period, most people believed owning was a better financial option than renting. And in a marketplace where home prices skyrocketed and an owner's equity soared, that was true. Then the housing bubble burst in 2008.

To me, one of the ugliest aspects of this situation is that so many people so badly wanted a piece of the American Dream that they made terrible financial decisions taking out huge, complex loans that they could never repay. The lenders who created these mortgages must shoulder even more of the blame for setting up such an untenable system, but in order to climb out of this mess, we need to think in terms of personal responsibility. At the end of the day, we have to understand what we're doing with our money and be responsible for making the best choices.

The rule of thumb used to be that you could only afford to buy a home that cost two and a half to three times your annual income. As interest rates came down, people's buying power increased . . . and so did the amount of money people were willing to borrow for a home. In the late 1980s, a client called worried that her daughter was about to buy a second home that she couldn't afford. I was quick to assure our client that no bank would lend out the money if her daughter didn't qualify for a loan. I was familiar with the daughter's finances and there was no way she could afford two homes. But she was approved and went ahead with the deal.

About a year later I had a call from the same client who told me another of her children was about to buy a home that she knew was beyond her reach. Again, I assured her that she wouldn't be able to get a loan if they couldn't afford the payments. (Talk about being a slow learner!) Well, would you believe that this loan was also approved?! As it turned out, the mortgage and property taxes were so unmanageable that they had to sell the house soon after they bought it. Thankfully they were able to get out from under the debt without having to take a loss on the deal.

I've been the beneficiary of easy access to credit, myself. When we decided it was time to cash out on our home equity and downsize to a smaller home, right before the subprime mortgage mess, we found a lovely home nearby. A builder expressed interest in paying us an unbelievable amount of money for our old home that they would tear down to build something bigger and better. Assuming that we would have a deal with the builder, I made an offer on the new home without making the purchase contingent on the sale of our old home. And then the whole real-estate bubble burst. The timing couldn't have been worse, but the banks were slow to respond to the crisis, and we could still get a bridge loan to go ahead with the transaction even though that meant we might be carrying two mortgages indefinitely . . . and that's exactly what we're doing. I thought I was doing something good for our family finances. Instead I've gouged our bottom line. We've been lucky: we have a lot of equity in the old home so if we wind up having to sell it at a fire sale we'll still be OK, and we've been able to rent the property to help defray the costs of the mortgage payments. But this kind of luck is rare.

So now, people are asking that question—rent or own? Often there isn't a choice. But if there is, people should consider some important questions. My dad, the banker, used to say that he thought it might be smarter to rent than to buy because you'd avoid the property taxes and maintenance costs that come with home ownership. But he died in 1987, before the run up in housing prices reached levels that my father could never have imagined. Anyone renting missed out on one of the greatest investments of the era. But even then, owning a home was not the only way to win. Renting can play an important role in building wealth. When the bubble burst, millions of homeowners found themselves "underwater," meaning that their mortgages were higher than the values of their homes.

In a February 2009 *Wall Street Journal* article, it was noted that "over the past 18 years, after-tax mortgage payments have averaged 26% more than rent payments." In fact, in 2006, at the height of the housing bubble, mortgage payments were as much as 66 percent more than rent payments. Needless to say, renting started to look like an enticing alternative. And sure enough, when the bubble burst, things changed rapidly. By the end of 2008, according to the *Journal*, the average monthly rent for the fifty largest metropolitan areas was $1,045, compared with the after-tax mortgage payments of $1,300 (assuming a rate of 5.5 percent on a thirty-year fixed mortgage). "That means mortgage payments averaged just 24% more than rent payments, the narrowest gap since 2001," according to the *Journal* article.

I'm not a financial adviser, but as an estate planning lawyer and a Wealth Watchers advocate, I can suggest some common-sense rules to follow, rules that my wealthiest clients seem to follow rigidly. First among these is that rent or mortgage payments must be affordable. Experts will tell you the mortgage you can afford is somewhere in the range of 25 to 35 percent of your gross income. According to an article in the *New York Times* in March 2009, financial advisers were suggesting that prospective home buyers use the old *28/36 rule*. That rule states that households should spend no more than 28 percent of their gross income on housing costs—including mortgage payments, property taxes, and insurance—and less than 36 percent on all debt including car payments, student loans, credit cards, and medical debt.

The article noted that the debate is still on about whether to base your calculations on your gross income or take-home pay. Of course, that's an easy one to resolve. In order to be really secure, use your take-home pay or net pay as the guide. That will assure that you stay out of trouble. It didn't surprise me to read that a whole lot of people have ignored the formula and are spending a far higher percentage of their income on mortgages. According to a 2007 American Community Survey from the Census Bureau, 38 percent of homeowners with mortgages spend more than 30 percent of their monthly gross income on housing costs. Incredibly, 12 percent of all owners, more than 9 million homeowners, spent "*more than half of their gross income on housing costs*." Wow.

What this tells me is that we've lost sight of the meaning and value of homeownership. By signing onto a mortgage that puts you into such a precarious financial position, you risk turning the American Dream into a nightmare.

Your home is going to be the roof over your head and your

biggest investment. But that doesn't mean that you have to buy the biggest home you can get a mortgage for. That kind of thinking got people in big trouble over the past few decades.

In my estate planning work, I've observed two fascinating things about wealthy people: First, they almost always buy rather than rent (not surprising) and second, our older clients try to pay for their homes as quickly as possible but only a handful of our younger clients seem anxious to pay off their mortgages. Even more interesting, most of our older clients own homes that are far more modest than what they can actually afford, but our younger clients are comfortable buying more upscale homes. I think people should have whatever kind of home they want as long as they understand the terms of their mortgage and are comfortable with all of the costs involved in owning that home. In the past, the idea of being mortgage free might have been scoffed at by money managers who applauded the tax deductions for interest payments and thought people should leverage their home equity and invest in the stock market. You'd always make more money in a hot stock market or other real estate investments. Now there's a simple word for people who have no mortgage: smart.

If you think about it, you can survive just about any economic crisis if you own your home outright. I understand that this is simply not realistic for most people and I'm not being judgmental. I don't own my own home outright so I'm in the same boat with most people. However, I've always made a point of considering any investment from both a short- and long-term perspective so that I could forecast as much as possible the best and worst-case scenarios that might arise. Trust me, I've made plenty of mistakes, but my goal is to encourage people to be smart with their money: to get a mortgage they can afford and pay it off in the shortest time period is a good goal.

Mortgages

According to *The National Strategy for Financial Literacy*, a booklet published by the U.S. Treasury Department and The Financial Literacy and Education Commission, "Technology and innovation have resulted in the creation of a plethora of mortgage loan products that are complex and possess features that may be inappropriate, very risky, and financially detrimental for some consumers, such as adjustable rate mortgages and interest-only loans where payment levels can change dramatically over the term of the loan." That was in 2006 and the warning came too late. Before the subprime lending fiasco, mortgages were reasonably easy to understand, and in fact they still can be. Generally, a buyer can apply for a either a fifteen-year or thirty-year fixed rate mortgage. There are also adjustable rate mortgages or ARMs added to the mix to give people who might be planning to live in a home for a shorter period of time a better short-term interest rate. In my estate planning practice, many of our clients had the shortest term mortgages they could get so they could own their homes outright in the fastest time. Others went with thirty-year mortgages but made extra payments which saved them money by shortening the length of time they held the loan.

Time is money. The longer it takes you to pay back your mortgage, the more money you will ultimately pay for your home. So it makes financial sense to try to get the shortest length mortgage you can afford or to make an extra payment when possible. Of course, along the way, you might be able to refinance in order to get a better interest rate or a shorter- or longer-term mortgage. You might even be able to pay down a larger portion of the mortgage. Most people refinance in order to take advantage of better options. I refinanced for the wrong reasons.

After my brain injury, our financial situation got so bad that we were forced to use home equity loans just to get by. Eventually, we had to refinance our home from a fifteen-year fixed rate to a thirty-year mortgage. It really killed me to do; making the switch added more than $200,000 to the cost of our loan! But we were in survival mode and had to do what we could to get by.

My advice to homebuyers, especially in a volatile and unpredictable market, is to consider exploring homes in a price range that will allow you to get by with a fifteen-year mortgage. The difference between what you should buy and what you want to buy may be eye-opening. The suitable home may be slightly smaller or in a different neighborhood, but small homes can be beautiful too and they grow even more attractive when you own them outright. I think we're beginning to see a movement of people deciding less is more.

Here are some examples from Bankrate.com of what your actual costs will be for a mortgage. I've included loans from $150,000 up to $1 million just to give you an idea what the monthly payments would be and how much you would pay in interest and principal over the life of the loan. The differences are dramatic:

Your Costs for a $150,000 Fixed-Rate Mortgage	15-year at 4.72 %	30-year at 5.09 %
Your monthly payment	$1,164	$ 814
Interest you'll pay during first 5 years	$31,079	$36,728
Interest you'll pay over full term of mortgage	$59,597	$142,861

The thirty-year mortgage would cost you $351 less each month. However, the total interest for the thirty-year mortgage would be $83,264 more than that of the fifteen-year mortgage.

Your Costs for a $300,000 Fixed-Rate Mortgage	15-year at 4.72 %	30-year at 5.09 %
Your monthly payment	$2,329	$1,627
Interest you'll pay during first 5 years	$62,158	$73,456
Interest you'll pay over full term of mortgage	$119,194	$285,722

The thirty-year mortgage would cost you $702 less each month. However, the total interest for the thirty-year mortgage would be $166,529 more than that of the fifteen-year mortgage.

Your Costs for a $600,000 Fixed-Rate Mortgage	15-Year at 5.93 %	30-Year at 6.88 %
Your monthly payment	$5,040	$3,944
Interest you'll pay during first 5 years	$157,883	$200,674
Interest You'll Pay Over Full Term of Mortgage	$307,286	$819,688

The thirty-year mortgage would cost you $1,097 less each month. However, the total interest for the thirty-year mortgage would be $512,402 more than that of the fifteen-year mortgage.

Your Costs for a $1 Million Fixed-Rate Mortgage	15-Year at 5.93 %	30-Year at 6.88 %
Your monthly payment	$8,401	$6,573
Interest you'll pay during first 5 years	$263,138	$334,456
Interest you'll pay over full term of mortgage	$512,143	$1,366,147

The thirty-year mortgage would cost you $1,828 less each month. However, the total interest for the thirty-year mortgage would be $854,003 more than that of the fifteen-year mortgage.

Wealth Watchers is a program that looks at the big picture and also details our daily costs. Let's look at the daily cost of each mortgage above. For the $150,000 mortgage, the cost per day would be $38.27 for the fifteen-year fixed rate and $26.76 per day for the thirty-year fixed rate. The fifteen-year mortgage will save you $83,264 in interest payments alone. Remember that the monthly payments are lower with the thirty-year rate but over the course of the loan, the interest you will pay is usually two to three times higher. Shorter is better, if you can.

For the $300,000 loan: $76.57 per day for the fifteen-year; $53.49 for the thirty-year but the fifteen-year mortgage will save you $166,529.

For the $600,000 loan: $165.70 per day for the fifteen-year; $129.67 for the thirty-year.

For the $1 million loan: $277.20 per day for the fifteen-year; $216.10 per day for the thirty-year.

You can also shorten the term of your mortgage by making biweekly instead of monthly payments. Essentially you would be making twenty-six payments a year instead of twelve. You may be able to cut six to eight years off your mortgage but you need to beware that some hefty fees may be involved. Make sure you do your homework before choosing this option.

When considering the whole picture, factor in property taxes and utilities. These will be significantly higher the more you pay for the home.

The interest saved by a fifteen-year mortgage, as opposed to a thirty-year, is astounding. So why don't more people make that choice? I can think of a few reasons. One is that many people want to be able to afford to buy a better home and they are willing to go with a thirty-year mortgage just to be able to afford their monthly payments. They may even plan on making extra payments toward principal down the road to shorten the length of their mortgage. The truth is that as a whole, we have become a country of people who don't like to delay gratification, and we're willing to pay for it.

People are also willing to go with a mortgage that will ultimately triple their interest expense because many don't plan on staying in their homes longer than a few years so they don't want to spend more each month to ultimately own their homes outright.

Maybe the biggest reason that people don't give much thought to the terms of their mortgage is that they don't explore all the options. This is where Wealth Watchers can make a real difference. Knowledge is power. The combination of financial knowledge and moral support can drastically improve the financial lives of millions of people.

Insurance

Most people become passive about their insurance. They either don't carry enough, or they don't take the time to review their existing policies to see if they could get the same coverage for less. I was one of those people who didn't pay attention to our insurance coverage. Even when a premium went up it didn't occur to me to ask why that had happened or to find out if there was a less expensive alternative. But all of that changed after *Wealth Watchers*. I looked at every expense in a new way. I was determined that we were going to get the biggest bang for our buck even if that meant having to change carriers every year. This philosophy might go against the grain of those who feel a sense of loyalty to their insurance agents. But loyalty in this case has a price. If you really care about getting the best value when it comes to insurance, you have to be willing to shop around. That doesn't mean your original agent will lose your business. In fact, I highly recommend going back to your agent to give him or her a chance to match a lower quote. You might be able to have the best of both worlds.

I'm not an investment adviser or an insurance expert, but as an estate planning attorney I've reviewed more than a thousand financial statements, and I've never come across a client who didn't have insurance. I'm not comfortable telling you what kind of insurance products you should have but I'll tell you what kind of insurance my family carries. We have health insurance, car insurance, life insurance, disability insurance, and home-owners insurance. The one policy that we don't have but that I wish we did is for long-term care. It seems that my brain injury is a "preexisting condition" that disqualifies me from being able to get long-term care insurance, but it is something I would encourage others to explore.

A few years ago, after reevaluating all of our insurance payments—automobile and homeowners—we were able to save $1,938 per year even though Andy had turned sixteen and was now on our policy. Had we not been paying attention, our rates would have actually increased by nearly $2,000 that year. We were able to cut costs by raising our car insurance deductibles to $500 and our homeowners insurance deductibles to $5,000.

I've been able to get reductions on all of our insurance with the exception of health care coverage. We were able to lower our annual insurance costs from $8,333 to $6,395. For so many Americans, the cost of insurance—particularly health insurance—has soared beyond reason.

Health Insurance

Nearly 50 million Americans have no health insurance and are forced to suffer from treatable maladies. Many Americans use the emergency room for minor health care problems because they know they won't be turned away if they are unable to pay. Medical expenses seem to hit the middle class the hardest. Medicaid takes care of people with few or no assets. But a medical setback for the middle class uninsured (or underinsured) can lead to bankruptcy. It is the middle class that stands to gain the most from much-needed health care reform.

It has become incredibly difficult to save money on health insurance in our nation. You can opt for a plan that has high deductibles and high co-payments but ceaseless increases in health insurance costs make it difficult to benefit from this strategy. There are so many factors involved, depending on your employer, your age, your medical history, and your family size. Any choices there are tend to be between bad and worse. Employers have steadily increased the percentage that employees must contribute each month for coverage. Massive layoffs in our workforce have forced millions to find alternative means of getting coverage.

And yet health insurance is vital not only to your physical but to your financial well-being. My brain injury provides a graphic example of this. If we hadn't had decent coverage when I was injured, my medical bills added to my lost income could have forced me into bankruptcy. There are carriers that offer cheaper plans if you are willing to make the sacrifices necessary—for example, if your longtime family physician isn't covered, you will need to switch doctors.

A professional colleague of mine who is self-employed fights an annual battle to find even remotely affordable health insurance. Without an employer to cover even part of the cost, he must pay the entire bill each month—now over $1,000—out-of-pocket. He has bounced from one plan to another, finding increasingly lower premiums and higher deductibles. One thing you can do if you are self-employed is join a local business organization—most states have them—which will make you eligible for health insurance at a group rate rather than at an individual rate. You must pay an annual membership fee but this will be small potatoes compared to your monthly savings. In fact your monthly dues are tax deductible, so your actual cost will be even lower.

Car Insurance

In states where the marketplace for automobile insurance is competitive, doing your homework and shopping for the lowest premiums is critical. One person I know in Massachusetts, where auto insurance rates had traditionally been set by the state, decided to get aggressive when the state laws changed recently. He called his insurance company and told them that he was planning to shop around and that he wanted to go over his plan in detail to see if there were potential savings. In a single ten-minute phone conversation, the company's rep found

Raising deductibles lowers insurance costs.
The type of car and home you own also affects your
insurance rates. Review all of your insurance policies to
make sure you're being smart. If you do raise your
deductibles, remember to set aside the savings
in your emergency savings account.

enough places for savings to reduce his monthly bill by $80! That's $960 in his pocket at the end of the year.

Before I became a Wealth Watcher, I never gave any thought as to how much it costs to insure a car. I always used *Consumer Reports* and did lots of research about a certain car's quality and reliability. But it never occurred to me to ask our insurance agent how much the insurance policy would cost for a specific car. In fact, the difference between insuring one model of car and another can be quite dramatic. It's well worth it to ask your insurance agency for insurance quotes on the makes and models of cars you're looking at before you buy one. Insurers look at things we would never consider such as how much it costs to replace a bumper on a particular model of car. Surprisingly, there is a huge variance between different models. And it might also surprise you to find out that some less expensive cars have higher bumper replacement costs than more expensive vehicles. Again, Wealth Watchers would never tell you what type of car you should buy or how much insurance you should carry. We just hope that you'll go through the process of buying and insuring a car with your eyes wide open. And remember that it pays to factor the cost of insurance into your car buying decision.

Life Insurance and Disability Insurance

Insurance is all about being prepared for the worst. We all want peace of mind and that's where insurance is worth its weight in gold. How many people could sleep at night if they didn't have homeowners insurance? There aren't many people who could afford to rebuild their home if it was destroyed by a fire.

How many of us could get by if we became disabled and could no longer work? Even when I found out that I had a brain injury I was sure that I would be better quickly. But a year after I'd been injured, I still had trouble working and my income had decreased significantly. We did what I'm sure most people would do and started to carry a balance on our credit card. Then we dipped into our home equity. Some time went by before I remembered that I'd bought disability insurance several years earlier. I'd associated it with cancer, for some reason, which may be why I didn't think of it immediately. But, of course, a brain injury also qualifies for disability benefits and the carrier honored my claim and backed up the payments to the time of the injury. Unfortunately I'd bought the policy when my income was much lower so it didn't cover all of my lost wages, but it was a big help. I would highly recommend that you talk to your insurance agent about disability insurance—and remember to update it if your salary increases. Just ask yourself this question. Can you afford to cover your living expenses if you can't work anymore? If not, then make the call.

How many families have enough money set aside to support themselves if the primary wage earner dies unexpectedly? It's so important to buy your life insurance while you're young and healthy. One major medical setback can send your premiums through the roof, or even worse, render you uninsurable after your term insurance expires. I'm not an expert in this field, but I've noticed that even our very wealthy clients carry life insurance. My guess is that they don't want their family members to have to liquidate assets if the markets are down.

A good insurance agent will be able to make a solid recommendation for how much and what type of life insurance a family might need. Again, it's important to talk to more than one agent. I'm in favor of loyalty but I'm more in favor of being an informed consumer.

"Term insurance" is relatively inexpensive while "whole" life insurance costs more. The big difference is that a term policy is only good for the actual term of the policy—typically twenty years. "Whole life insurance" is a permanent insurance policy that can't be revoked if you develop a medical condition that might otherwise make you uninsurable. There's also something called "universal life insurance" which is a blend of term and whole life insurance.

Many employers have group plans but they usually provide only a nominal amount of term life insurance coverage and the insurance is only good as long as you're employed by that company. If you developed cancer and had to leave that company it would be extremely tough to get any type of coverage.

In difficult times, life insurance is seen as expendable. Understandably, if there's a choice between putting food on the table and having life insurance, people choose food on the table. But it would be reckless to leave behind a young family without a way to make ends meet. It's an everyday tragedy that can be avoided by having life insurance.

The proceeds from my life insurance will be payable to a trust that will set aside something for Eddie and Andy as well as give Dan enough money to pay off our mortgage and cover the cost of raising KC and sending her to college. Anything that is left after Dan is gone will be held in separate but equal trust accounts for all of our children

Keep in mind that I am completely biased in this area, but this is where the cost of an estate planning attorney is a solid investment. Our area of law concerns itself entirely with giving people peace of mind.

SEMI-FIXED EXPENSES

Transportation

As of 2006, there were more than 250 million registered passenger vehicles on the road in the United States, and the number of cars and trucks far outpaces the number of licensed drivers. This recession has given us the first drop in newly registered vehicles since 1960. The average age of these vehicles has crept up as people have delayed purchasing new ones. And keeping a car on the road is not an inexpensive proposition, especially when gasoline prices soar as they did in the summer of 2008. For some families the cost of transportation—including maintenance—can make up 15 percent of the overall budget.

Leasing a Car vs. Owning

As a Wealth Watcher, I favor owning a car over leasing one. There are pros and cons to both owning and leasing, though leasing seems to have grown more expensive in recent years as car companies have gotten into trouble. In order to get a favorable monthly rate in a lease, you have to put down some cash up front—anywhere from $1,000 to $3,000 or more depending upon how expensive the vehicle is. Calculating a lease payment involves knowing the manufacturer's recommended sticker price, the interest rate of the lease, the length of the lease (twenty-four months, thirty-six months), and the residual value of the car. The good thing about a lease is that the resulting monthly payment is usually quite a bit less than the monthly payment on a car loan. Leasing has allowed many to drive much nicer cars than they can afford to buy for a few years before they turn them in and start the process all over again. Unfortunately, if you end the lease without rolling into a new lease, you essentially walk away empty-handed, having invested many thousands of dollars into "renting" a car for a few years. You also have to factor in sales taxes, excise taxes in some states, and the penalty of higher insurance costs for driving brand new cars.

Owning a vehicle, depending on make and model and year, is also a mixed bag. When you purchase a car, its value declines the minute you drive it off the dealer's lot. If you are taking a loan, the monthly payments can be steep and you incur all the extra costs you would for a leased car including sales taxes, excise taxes, and higher insurance costs. Maintenance costs tend to increase as the car gets older and warranties expire. Some people just like to own their own cars, plain and simple . . . and if you own a vehicle, it is an asset on your balance sheet. A leased car is not.

Whatever you do, make sure you do your homework. My two favorite resources for buying a car are Consumer Reports and Edmunds.com. Edmunds is easy to access and I'd recommend going to the site. They offer a feature called "The True Cost to Own," that lets you know how much it costs to drive a certain make of car per mile over a five-year period. It factors in depreciation, financing, insurance, taxes and fees, fuel, maintenance, and repairs. You can't go by the sticker price alone.

Here are some examples:

- A 2009 Mustang convertible had an MSRP of $25,255 but the True Cost to Own was listed as $47,441 over five years, or 63 cents per mile.
- A 2009 Volkswagon Beetle had an MSRP of $25,990 but the TCTO was $42,452 over five years, or 57 cents per mile
- A 2009 Toyota Prius hybrid was listed at $22,000 and the TCTO was $33,252 over five years, just 44 cents a mile.
- A 2009 Kia Optima sold for $17,148 but the TCTO jumped to $38,011 or 51 cents per mile.

The Kia is good example of a car that has a lower purchase price but may actually wind up costing more than a more expensive car because it may be more costly to repair. There are so many hidden costs to car ownership that I often envy friends who live in big cities and don't own a car at all. Public transportation has Wealth Watchers written all over it. Commuting by public transportation is much cheaper than commuting in your car—gasoline and tolls aside, just think about the cost of parking if you live in a major city! While it's convenient to drive to work, especially if you are commuting from the suburbs, public transportation is always a huge cost saver.

Smart Wealth Watchers consider another aspect of ownership: which cars keep their value over time. As new car sales plummeted, in the economic downturn, cost conscious drivers not only began keeping their vehicles on the road far longer, they bought more used cars. The value of a given car becomes even more important when it's bought used. But there are many resources to help buyers calculate. Cars.com indicates that in 2009 the Mini-Cooper had retained 68 percent of its value over three years. Over that same period, the Cadillac DTS had retained just a 23 percent resale value. There are so many variables in this equation that I won't even try to go into them here. I only want to encourage you to do your homework and understand how far apart the extremes of depreciation are.

I found a great list posted on Edmunds.com entitled "A Cheapskate's Top 10 Money-Saving Ideas for Car Owners" by Mac Demere. Mac points out that we shouldn't "laugh at the guy driving the 15-year-old beater. He might be on his way to becoming a millionaire."

His list of money-saving ideas includes driving rather than flying, letting the "other guy" take the hit, and driving your car forever. This all makes great sense:

- If you're traveling 500 miles or less, it's just not worth it to fly. When you consider the travel time to the airport, the cost of parking or transportation to the airport, getting through security, possible delays due to any number of reasons, along with the cost of transportation from the arrival airport to your ultimate destination, you're most likely going to come out ahead of the game no matter how you slice it if you drive instead of fly.
- Why buy something that depreciates as much as 25 percent the minute you own it? A car that is two or three years old can still retain most of its value.
- An older car may not be as fashionable, but wouldn't it be nice to pay off your car and have a few years without car payments? Car insurance will be less expensive on a used car than on the newest model. You can also put off paying the sales tax incurred every time you buy a new car.

One thing that Wealth Watchers should do is track gasoline purchases in their journals. It was amazing to see how people cut back on their driving when gasoline prices skyrocketed and then picked right back up when the prices came down. You can add a lot of discipline to your driving habits if you pay attention to what each mile costs you. When the cost of gas doubled in 2008, Dan and I switched cars. He usually does a lot more driving than I do and he has a minivan to haul shot-putters and discus throwers to track meets along with team equipment. I have a hybrid which is only big enough to hold our family. When we switched, it was summer and track season was over, so the trade worked. When gas prices dropped, we switched again.

Child Care

Child care is the fourth largest expense in our budget. And it's what keeps many people from getting ahead when their kids are young. Face it, children are expensive. When you calculate the cost of raising a child from birth to college graduation, it can come to well over $300,000! From a Wealth Watchers point of view, that is about $37 a day! But for most of us, this is a financial burden we take on with pleasure. Our children are priceless, and we tend not to think about these costs as anything but essential.

Nonetheless, child care costs can exact a real toll on families, especially these days. Day care costs have soared over the years. According to a report from the National Association of Child Care Resource and Referral Agencies in July 2008 (www.naccrra.org), the price of child care is rising faster than the average rate of inflation. The report provides the typical prices of child care for infants and four-year-olds in day care centers and family child care homes in each state. In one year, the average cost of these services rose 6.5 percent, almost twice the rate of inflation.

The report pointed out that in 2007, the average price of full-time care for an infant in a center was as high as $14,591 ($40 a day x 365). Parents paid up to $10,787 a year for a four-year-old in a center ($30 a day x 365). For home child care, the costs were slightly lower but many of those providers are unlicensed.

Clearly, quality child care is essential, but it isn't cheap. In a perfect working world, a company would offer on-site day care for infants and toddlers and a flexible work schedule so that employees with school-age children could work during school hours and then go home. I'm sure some progressive companies have done this. But in a tough economy, these types of benefits are often eliminated first.

Economic reality doesn't change one thing: There is nothing better than being able to drop off your kids and pick them up from school without having the expense or worry of after-school care. For most people, this is a difficult or impossible dream. But there are often cheaper alternatives. We're lucky to have a strong YMCA in our town that actually provides before and after-school care at each of the elementary schools. KC liked it so much that she used to get mad if we picked her up too early from the after-school Y program. The program cost $345 per month in 2006.

My family has run the gamut of child care options from using a service called Naperville Nannies that provided live-in or day nannies to day care, which—aside from family babysitting—actually wound up being the better option. Things worked best for us when I could fit all of my work into the hours of the school day, because, until KC came along, we were able to eliminate the cost of child care from our budget. If you're part of a two-income couple and have benefits at both jobs, you might be able to convince one of your employers to drop benefits in exchange for a more flexible work schedule. Some employers are open to this. After KC was born, I went from working five to six days a week to working just two and a half days each week. Our child care costs were less than half of what they would have been if I had been working full time. The big surprise was that even though I'd decreased my hours, my income increased! When you have to make hay in a shorter amount of sunshine, you don't waste time.

I've never hired an au pair, but this can be an affordable, compelling option for families. There are some great au pair agencies and programs monitored by the U.S. State Department, and they are very affordable, especially for families with more than one child. The average weekly cost of au pair care averages about $320 regardless of the number of children in the family, far less than parents might pay for day care or for a nanny. This is comparable to the $14,591 a year spent by families sending just one child to a day care center. For families with two or more children, au pair child care makes the most sense financially.

College

It's fair to say that the cost of college in America has shot into the stratosphere. Most private, four-year colleges cost close to or more than $50,000 a year for tuition, room and board, and fees. The very idea that you can spend $200,000 for an undergraduate degree boggles the mind. Public colleges are raising their prices as well, forcing many families to take out massive student loans, home equity loans, or find alternatives to colleges such as vocational schools or even studying in another country where the costs may be far lower.

There are no easy solutions to this costly problem, especially for middle-class families that make too much to qualify for significant financial aid but too little to afford the staggering costs. Asking a college student to graduate with the burden of tens of thousands of dollars in student loans just seems cruel and counterproductive to me.

The costs are worth looking at from a Wealth Watchers perspective. For example, the estimated cost of tuition, fees, books, room and board at Northwestern University in the 2009–2010 school year was $53,854 or $147.55 per day (365 days a year). At a state school, like the University of Illinois, those same costs for a resident of Illinois were $25,654 or $70.28 a day, a significant difference. And at our local community college, the College of DuPage, in 2009–2010, the estimated cost of attending school full time was $5,086 or $13.93 per day—not including living expenses.

The College of DuPage may not seem to be in the same academic league as an elite private university, but there is real value in taking lower-level courses at a community college and then transferring to the college of your choice to get your undergraduate degree. Good classes and teachers are where you find them. There has been a flood of applications to state colleges around the country in the past year. Clearly the recession has forced students and their families to rethink their priorities and goals. If you can get a quality educational experience at a state university for a fraction of the cost, it seems foolish to not consider that option.

When my oldest son Eddie went off to college in 2002, he spent his first two years at Scottsdale Community College in Arizona. The first year, we had to pay out-of-state tuition along with the cost of an apartment. But the next year, he was eligible for in-state tuition. It was a very cost effective way to attend college. His second year at Scottsdale, tuition cost $1,500 and another $8,000 for room, board, and books. From a Wealth Watchers point of view, it cost us $26 a day.

But we weren't off the hook. Eddie chose to spend his final two years at Miami University of Ohio where his tuition was around $22,000, his room and board another $8,000. That increased the daily total to $82 . . . 365 days a year! And that sounds like a bargain compared to today's average tuition!

Needless to say, I'm a big fan of community colleges. As the recession deepened and more people lost their jobs, the road to four-year, private college closed for many qualified students. Even if many wanted to borrow the money, there weren't enough loans available to cover the soaring costs. The community college alternative is a good one because most have excellent professors, wide course selection, and smaller classes than large universities.

A parent can try to get a job at a college or university. Most jobs in academia offer tuition assistance for employees, their spouses and their dependent children, as much as an 85 percent discount! A student willing to live at home might get an education at an elite university for $5,714 a year! How amazing to get a degree for 85% off!

The rising cost of college has brought along with it the spectre of terrible debt. Though most financial advisers suggest that a student not accrue more loans than would equal a year's salary, this is a difficult line to walk. According to an article in the *New York Times* in April 2009, about two-thirds of students graduating in the spring of 2009 (that's an estimated 1.8 million students) will have loans to repay. And according to FinAid.org, the average debt among graduating seniors is $22,500! One graduate mentioned in the *Times* owed $150,000! Before he even hits the workforce he will owe $1,500 a month. It's no surprise the student loan default rate is rising.

Contemplating these massive, fixed expenses can be overwhelming. In Chapter 5, we will focus on discretionary spending, which is at the heart of the Wealth Watchers formula. In order to offset the burden of our fixed costs, we need to take charge and invent creative ways to find and sustain our DDI.

CHAPTER FIVE

Discretionary Spending

I'm often asked if the Wealth Watchers philosophy—that we should keep track of our daily discretionary spending—is too much of a burden. Why would you give up the ease and efficiency of simply swiping a credit or debit card and walking away with your purchase? But this efficiency is the problem. The various advancements in the financial services industry seem to have had an unintended consequence: they've allowed us to skip an important step in the decision process involved in making a purchase. In the name of adding ease and efficiency to a transaction, these cards have stolen our moment to "think before we spend."

Sure, writing down everything you spend is an effort. But it's an effort that will help improve your bottom line. It's an effort that your children will notice. It's an effort that will help you understand that every day and every dollar really do make a difference.

At Weight Watchers, our leader, Betty Bennett, used to have this saying. "Nothing tastes as good as being thin makes you feel." When it comes to money, I've found that no "purchase" feels as good as being in control of my money. Writing down everything I ate made it much simpler to lose weight just as writing down everything I spend has made it possible for us to vastly improve our bottom line.

After starting the Weight Watchers program, I wouldn't grab

a handful of M&Ms from the candy dish in our office. Not only would it have been a waste of calories, I would have had to take time to write down that I ate something in my Weight Watchers journal. That added step made me think before I ate. Was it a pain? Well, a little. But it was worth it to get back to my old weight. When it comes to money, the same principle applies. Something as trivial as taking a moment to write down a purchase can actually change the way you shop. You won't want to look back at your journal and see that you wasted money. And the result is that you too can see your bottom line improve

There is also a disconnect between what people think they have spent and what they have actually spent. If you've ever been surprised by the balance due on your credit card statement at the end of the month then you know what I mean. Many people don't seem to have any idea how much money they have spent until the statement arrives . . . just as many people can't understand why they are overweight.

If you want to change your financial life, you can't just talk about it. You have to take action. So if you really care about money, you need to know your numbers. You need to understand down to the day what you can spend without going into debt. You need to track all of your spending for at least a month or two. And if you try it, you might find that it is not only far less of a burden than you'd feared, but that the rewards are many, not just in saving money, but in feeling in control of your finances.

Knowing your fixed expenses is pretty easy. The bills, which many of us pay online or through auto-pay these days, are often simple to track. This is true even of bills that are semi-fixed and fluctuate occasionally. But for discretionary spending, most people have no idea how much or how little they are spending each month or how quickly the little things add up.

Listen to James, a writer in Massachusetts, who kept a daily spending journal for more than eight years, long before Wealth Watchers even got started:

"I'd heard someone on a talk show discussing their monthly expenses and it occurred to me that I had no idea what we spent every month. Was it $4,000 or $6,000? Did we spend $100 a week on food or $200? I decided to track it and I set up a hand-written journal and started putting in everything my wife and I spent each day. We would sit down every night and I'd ask my wife for any credit card receipts she had and to tell me how much cash she had spent and on what. I have to say that Lisa didn't have a particular interest in doing this but she went along with it. She is not very organized about what she spends so every night I had to interview her. One thing that was important was to not be overbearing about it. I didn't push for every pack of gum because it would turn her off.

"We had our update every night so we didn't forget cash purchases. I set everything up by categories—entertainment, clothes, gifts, vacation, restaurants, charities, gasoline, car maintenance, doctor visits, prescriptions, and miscellaneous for things that didn't fit into a category. All these things were highly variable. I kept track of fixed expenses as well but most of those I knew ahead of time. But things like utilities can vary quite a bit from month to month and season to season. It helped to track those every month in order to compare how much you spent the year before.

"I know it sounds pretty anal but it really wasn't hard to do. Once you start, it becomes a habit. I learned some very interesting things. At the end of each month, I could see if we had spent too much on eating out, given too much or not enough to charity. The best thing it did was make us realize that every time you reached for your wallet, you'd be recording it. It made us ask ourselves, 'Do we really want to spend this or not.' In good times, when you have a nice income and money is coming in, you don't even think about it. 'Five or ten dollars won't break me.' But you realize how quickly things add up.

"When you do it every month, you start to realize how many expenses are not under your control. So you have to focus on those things you can control, like eating out, shopping for clothes, gas, vacations, entertainment . . . all areas you have an effect on. And for us, it had an impact on our behavior. We shopped at a cheaper supermarket. We would find gas stations with cheaper prices. We cut down on eating out.

"It not only helps you save money, it brings you back to, is it worth it? It makes you really focus on the value of money. We lose that sometimes. We say 'I have it, I deserve it, why not?' For us, spending had to pass a certain threshold. Do we really want to spend this? For example, at a restaurant, you order a glass of wine and it costs $7 or $8 or more. Do you really want that or would you rather spend the money on something else? At a wine store, you can buy a nice bottle of wine for $10! Maybe you'd enjoy the wine at home and you get a lot more for your money.

"The most important thing it does is give you a real sense of controlling your expenditures. It is very empowering. You realize that with maybe 40 percent of your expenditures you have a choice about whether to spend or not, and how to spend it. We felt like we were eliminating waste and we felt better about what we were spending our money on. We don't mind spending money but we want to know that we are getting value and enjoyment out of it, not just spending out of habit. We're so influenced by advertising and marketing, and by doing this we had more control over things we purchased. It's a great way to balance that buying and selling relationship.

> **"Man is rarely so harmlessly occupied
> as when making money."**
> *John Stuart Mill.*
>
> I think this should be updated to say that people are rarely so
> harmlessly occupied as when making money or enjoying life at
> home. Our home should be the place we choose to be . . . not
> the place we go shopping to get away from.

"You also recognize the relationship between the work you do
that produces that income and how you use that income. Sometimes I would think, do we really want to work for three hours
to earn the money to buy that sweater or go out to eat? Keeping
track reframes the relationship between work and spending."

THE EPIPHANY OF JOURNALING

What James experienced was the epiphany that I've heard
echoed by almost all the people who have tried Wealth Watchers. By tracking your discretionary spending every day, you
unleash the power of 365, the sense of knowing in detail what
you have, what you are spending on a daily basis, and how
important it is to pay attention to every dollar and every day.
Know what you have, know what you need, know what you can
live without.

In Chapter 4, we focused on fixed and semi-fixed expenses.
Here let's look at the categories that include your daily disposable income or DDI.

At Wealth Watchers, we've broken the discussion about DDI into four categories: essential purchases; big ticket/infrequent spending; small item/entertainment/social expenses, and the wish list. What these categories have in common are countless opportunities for ways to spend better, smarter, and more carefully so that savings occur spontaneously. There's no secret sauce or magic here, just a very potent combination of desire and discipline which I've found is an unbeatable way to succeed in almost anything in life.

ESSENTIAL PURCHASES

Food

Wealth Watchers Approach: *Food, while a necessity, is a discretionary expense. Do not go food shopping without a list.*

As I've said, it is no coincidence that the credit crisis and the obesity crisis in our country seem to have traveled on parallel paths. There are so many psychological connections between overspending and overeating. For me, it is a particularly vulnerable area because I dislike grocery shopping and I don't like to cook. I like to take the easy way out by eating at restaurants or bringing home takeout. That saves unwanted time in the kitchen but it is not cheap. Ultimately, our food bill is roughly $150 each week and that's on top of our restaurant bill of around $100 each week which means we spend around $1,000 a month on food. Next to our mortgage, food is the most expensive item in our budget.

My aversion to the supermarket led me to try my hand at shopping online even though there is a $7 delivery fee. I figured that it would save me an hour of my time, not to mention the aggravation, and I'd heard that people tend to spend less money when they shop for groceries online. Unfortunately, that wasn't my experience. My online order came to $180 and that was without any impulse purchases. I rechecked my order before it was shipped and cut $50 from my shopping list. But eventually I gave up grocery shopping online because the delivery fee was raised to $10 and I'd found better deals in the store than online.

In 2007, Dan and I decided to use only cash for all purchases except gasoline and travel. It was a major pain, but it taught us a good deal about the way we spend money. When I went grocery shopping, I took $150 and really stuck to the basics. I was able to shop for $106 for a week but that was only because Dan takes KC out to eat on Thursday and we order pizza and bring it home on Fridays. I stuck with the cash-only method for as long as I could stand it. With my brain injury, I was always forgetting to stop at the ATM for cash and constantly found myself embarrassingly shorthanded at lunch with friends or business colleagues. I came away from our experiment certain that one has to find a balance between cards and cash. But this didn't help with my food bills.

I decided I could cook more, spending money wisely on groceries, but I couldn't eliminate restaurant bills entirely. It certainly blew my mind to learn that in the United States, 40 percent of all food spending is for eating outside the home. You can truly save thousands of dollars each year by eating at home. Like I said, it's your choice. We all have routines that enrich our lives and those are tough to give up.

The Corner Bakery is one of our favorite places to eat out, and it used to be within walking distance of our home. It has a menu loaded with healthy dishes and there is no tipping, which saves us 20 percent on the bill (and I don't mean to imply that you should stiff the servers with a small tip). Being a Wealth Watcher doesn't mean taking something away from a hardworking employee. On weekends, Dan used to go to the Corner Bakery first thing in the morning and bring back a pumpkin muffin and a cookie for KC, a chocolate muffin for Andy, a cinnamon roll for Eddie, a large iced tea for himself, and Starbucks coffee for me. (I know, not a very Weight Watchers [or Wealth Watchers!] thing to do!) A typical weekend morning used to cost at least $18 ($18 x 104 weekend mornings is $1,872). But one Saturday morning, I made pumpkin muffins and that was our breakfast. The mix costs less than $3 and there were enough muffins left over for the next day. Dan made his own iced tea and I skipped the coffee. KC said my muffins were better than the Corner Bakery's and we saved at least $15 ($15 x 104 is $1,560).

I think the people at the Corner Bakery must think Dan is a single father. I usually work late on Thursdays and Dan always takes KC there for dinner that night. One year he went there, on average, three times a week. More than 150 times! He's such a loyal customer that when he went to Europe for ten days he sent a post card to the employees telling them that he hoped they wouldn't go under while he was gone. But those meals and drinks cost an average of $8 per person, a far higher sum than we would have spent had we cooked dinner on those nights.

We have other, similar, rituals, and I'll bet your family does as well. As I said, Friday night is pizza night. We like to rent a movie and order a pizza. The kids used to prefer Blockbuster because it has a great selection but the movies there are more than $4 each ($4 x 52 = $208 or for two movies $8 x 52 = $416). I can get movies from the public library for free or for $1, which amounts to a significant savings over the course of a year. Also, I can pick up the pizza myself, which saves $6 in delivery fees and tips ($6 x 52 = $312). Now, there are so many low-cost

> Ben Franklin was correct about the small leaks.
> If you pay attention, you'll find your leak. It could be
> in your daily habits or it could be in your monthly bills. It
> could be the lights you leave on or the thermostat
> that should be adjusted . . . or the cable plan that could
> be less expensive. When you watch the little things,
> everything else falls into place.

options for watching movies at home—from Netflix (as low as $4.99 a month to rent two videos) to the On Demand feature on many cable television systems (which offer free and low-cost films)—that it becomes harder to justify the cost of going to a movie theater.

Wednesday used to be Dunkin' Donuts day. During the school year, we'd break up the week by stopping at Dunkin' Donuts on our way to drop Andy off at school. Our usual order would come to around $8 ($8 x 36 weeks of school = $288). We had a family vote whether or not it was worth it to spend nearly $300 on the Dunkin' Donuts tradition. Dunkin' Donuts won unanimously (only because we didn't allow Dan to vote). We all love traditions and there are some decisions to be made—quality of life versus savings—in your quest for financial security.

Jane, a Wealth Watchers member, told us that her husband was thrilled that she was finally trying to be careful with money. She also felt that she was setting a good example for her daughter by joining Wealth Watchers. But she told us an enlightening story. When she came to her first Wealth Watchers meeting, she had with her a cup of Starbucks coffee, and she acknowledged that it cost $3. But she explained that this didn't feel wasteful to her at all. On the contrary, Jane is a cancer survivor, and when she was going through chemotherapy treatments, the staff at Starbucks became like a support group for her. They even kept special hormone-free milk in the refrigerator for her coffee. They called it "Jane's milk" and no one else was allowed to use it. Needless to say, that was $3 well spent!

As you can see, Wealth Watchers would never tell you how to spend your discretionary income. One person's luxury is another's necessity. Weight Watchers would never tell someone not to eat something. They would just encourage you to plan for it by cutting the calories at another meal. I think the same thing is true with money. If we handle our money with care, we can have most of the things we want. Sometimes we are forced to cut back on things that we enjoy, but if we plan for them, we can always look forward to a time when we will be able to afford them again. And they will be that much better for having been absent. "It's not in the family budget" is good for children to hear. This kind of small, regular sacrifice can go a long way toward establishing your family values. Ben Franklin was correct. "Small leaks" do "sink great ships." I've seen first hand how holding back on small expenditures has saved my family thousands of dollars every year. If people started doing this while they were young they could even set aside sizable savings for an emergency. There might be something to the idea that if you're prepared for the worst it won't happen . . . and if it does, then at least you're able to weather the storm.

The $50 Weekly Grocery Bill

Carol Vander Wilt, the first guest on our *Wealth Watchers* cable television show, told us how she decided around ten years ago that people were spending far too much on groceries and set out to cut her own grocery bill. She established an ambitious goal: to *spend no more than $50 a week to feed her husband and two growing boys*. Incredibly, she accomplished her goal by sticking to a disciplined plan for food shopping. And it wasn't even that difficult.

"No matter what you are trying to accomplish, the first rule is to be disciplined," Carol says. "You are the boss. Another rule: always go shopping alone. Don't bring your spouse or children. It will save you a lot of money. The kids are always grabbing impulse items and throwing them in the shopping cart. I used to bring my husband sometimes and I noticed that the basket was always filled with expensive prepared food and junk we shouldn't have been eating anyway. And it cost a fortune. One time I actually counted what he bought and it came to $37! And it was stuff I would never buy. "Next, I always made a shopping list, and I stuck to it. I didn't just grab impulse items as I went through the store. In fact, I never brought along recipes. That is a surefire way to blow your budget. I was always very creative when I got home. I looked at what I had and searched through my cookbooks to find recipes and get ideas. It actually became a lot of fun. If I found chicken on sale, I'd buy it and make a nice chicken dish for dinner.

"I never clipped coupons but I did look at the food advertisements in the newspaper each week. They came out on Thursday. And I only bought what was on sale. This included staples like soap and toilet paper. I shopped at two stores which are two miles apart. It only took one hour a week, and I never went back to the store during the same week. I found some good discount grocery stores and shopped at those.

"We never splurged on dessert. We didn't care for dessert. I liked salads. And we would go out for dinner maybe once a week. It really wasn't hard at all. It did take a few years to develop the technique but now that my kids are grown, I am reaping the rewards. I had trained myself to shop carefully so today, it is actually difficult to spend a lot of money. Old habits are hard to break. It was not a miracle. It was all about discipline.

"I started doing this when my boys were young and I saved about $150 a week, which over ten years amounted to savings of about $78,000! That's a lot of money. And nobody went hungry, believe me. The boys always had good home-cooked meals. I always packed their lunch for school. They didn't mind. In fact, it must have worked pretty well. My youngest son is six feet seven inches tall!"

I'm sure there are plenty of people out there who will roll their eyes at Carol's regimen. But imagine how good it feels to know that you've saved $78,000 over the years on an essential expense such as food. That's more than a down payment on a nice home. There are millions of people who have Carol's kind of discipline, many out of necessity, and we could all learn from that kind of wealth watching. Especially me.

The old me, prior to Wealth Watchers, used to go grocery shopping without any thought to how much money I was spending. I didn't have a shopping list, a menu, or a budget. But as soon as I realized that we shouldn't spend more money than we had, I thought twice about everything we spent money on, including groceries. For the first time in my life I created a menu plan, then based our shopping list on that. Besides food and beverages I usually wind up buying shampoo, toothpaste, laundry detergent, cleaning products, and the like—I still categorize these items as groceries. Of course, any shopper worth her salt is aware that these sundry household items can be bought for far less and in larger quantities at places like Costco, BJ's, or Walmart.

What I Spend

The groceries I buy cover sixteen meals for three people, a total of forty-eight meals per week. The cost is around $3 per person per meal. It's actually a little less than this since my groceries include things like shampoo and laundry detergent. When we eat out, the bill is typically around $8 per person. Given our usual eating out rituals, that is four meals that I don't make at home. Thus our average restaurant bill is approximately $96 a week. Compare that to the $36 it costs to eat at home . . . Wow! What a difference!

Breakfast

Dan and I have cereal or toast for breakfast most mornings and KC has pancakes and a banana three days a week, cereal two days a week, and we all have homemade waffles or pumpkin muffins along with scrambled eggs on Saturday and Sunday mornings. I know so many people who splurge on weekend mornings like we used to, going out for big breakfasts at local diners or chains like Denny's and IHOP, bringing home a dozen hot bagels and fresh cream cheese spreads, or driving out to a country inn for a nice buffet brunch. Trust me, I love these fun breakfasts as much as anyone but for a family of four, a breakfast at IHOP or a local diner can easily cost $60 with tax and tip. If you decided not to do that every Sunday (52 x $60 = $3,120), you would save lots of money

Lunch

During the week, Dan and KC pack a lunch. It's so much better and cheaper than most school cafeteria food. I usually have peanut butter and crackers at the office for lunch. Our group will usually bring in carry-out for lunch once a week. Occasionally I'll have a business lunch, or I'll meet a friend for lunch. Weekend lunches aren't as easy. We're usually out and about so we're more likely than not to eat fast food or go to a restaurant. The convenience of going out for lunch on the weekends with Dan and KC winds up costing anywhere between $15 for fast food and up to $40 if we go to a restaurant and order drinks. Eating at home or packing a lunch would cost less than $10. But I don't feel too bad about our occasional trips to a restaurant. That may be my favorite way to contribute to our economy.

Dinner

I cook dinner Sunday night through Wednesday night. On Thursday Dan either stops by The Corner Bakery on his way home from work and brings home dinner or takes KC for dinner at the restaurant. Friday is Pizza Night and Saturday night is usually "every man for himself." Normally this means leftovers. But the bright side is that they don't cost a thing!

Miscellaneous

We go through three to four gallons of milk and two two-liter bottles of soft drinks each week. Our alcohol intake fluctuates depending upon whether or not we have company during the week, but we probably consume (with friends) two bottles of wine and about a dozen bottles of beer each week. Dan used to spend close to $6 a day on iced tea but now we buy loose tea for $8 a pouch, which makes ten large glasses of tea and I brew a pot each day in our coffee maker. So if you do the math ($6 x 30 days = $180 a month versus 80 cents x 30 days or $24 a month) that's a significant savings. I also make coffee at home or I'll have coffee once I get to the office. Starbucks, which I love, is now an occasional treat.

In the spirit of saving money I actually signed up for a cooking class through the Naperville Park District. Everyone in the class was assigned a dish to make and all of the ingredients were provided. The recipe assigned to me was for some sort of soufflé and since it took the longest to prepare, it was the last dish to be served to the group. When the instructor flipped my creation onto the serving plate, instead of sitting up proudly like a soufflé should, it slid off the plate like an octopus on an ice skating rink. She said she had never seen anything like that happen before. I think she was trying to be nice. If nothing else, it validated my opinion of my own cooking skills.

In better financial days, we used to have meals made for us by a woman in our town who loved to cook. It wasn't expensive and with my law practice to run and kids to raise, it actually made good economic sense to pay someone else to do something I wasn't good at anyway. In this economy, it becomes harder to justify such an expense, and I just need to find the discipline to make cooking healthy meals at home a priority. Maybe I should start DVRing Rachael Ray to learn some quick and easy recipes that even I can't screw up.

Coupons

Even though Carol was able to feed a family of four on $50 a week without clipping coupons, we shouldn't ignore the stories from around the country in which people have saved thousands of dollars every year by clipping coupons. Several of our millionaire law clients are religious about using coupons when they grocery shop. The Internet is full of advice about making the most of coupon clipping: Grocerycouponguide.com, estimates that there are $360 billion worth of grocery coupons floating out there and that people who actively clip and use them can shave between 30 and 50 percent off their weekly grocery bill. Like Carol, I've always ignored the coupon route but you can't ignore the real savings available if you are willing to make the effort.

Clothing

Wealth Watchers Principle: *Do a wardrobe inventory before you go shopping. Beware of the temptation to save money by buying discounted items. This is especially true now that a bad economy has forced many retailers to reduce the price of merchandise. Remember that you can go broke trying to save money.*

Most of us already have enough clothes, so really what we should be talking about here is clothing for growing children, or clothing for a career transition. But we can't disregard the elephant in the room. Many of us just like to shop and can't ignore the siren call of a great sale. If you're reading this book and you hate to shop, my guess is that you are a natural born Wealth Watcher. For the rest of us, this is an area where we can strategize to keep ourselves from going broke (especially by pretending to save money at sales).

Think about this: According to Jeff Yeager, author of *The Ultimate Cheapskate's Road Map to True Riches*, fewer than 2 percent of clothes that we Americans throw away are actually worn out. Now I'm very fashion conscious so I understand the desire to avoid wearing a blouse you bought when Reagan was in the White House. But with the average family spending nearly $2,000 a year on clothes, this is a great place to employ your Wealth Watchers skills.

> A friend of mine says,
> "No sale is a bargain if you didn't need the item,"
> because you can go broke saving money.

Here's a list of the things I've picked up from other Wealth Watchers that we should think about when it comes to clothing.

1. **Don't spend more money than you have.** If you buy something for 85 percent off the retail price, but put it on a credit card and wind up paying for it over time, you could find yourself actually spending the retail price many times over!

2. As with groceries, **don't shop without a list.**

3. **Go through your wardrobe** before you go shopping. Recently, a woman told me that she has sixteen pairs of black pants in her closet. Another woman told me she has thirty pairs of blue jeans.

4. **Clean out your closets and drawers.** If it doesn't fit and it's not going to fit any time soon, then donate or sell the item. If you don't wear it and you're not going to wear it any time soon, then it goes in the donate or sell pile unless it's something you absolutely love and can't part with. Yes, I realize that is a contradiction but we all have some item we cherish, whether it's a Joe Montana football jersey or a Dior gown that we don't wear. I've read that you should go through your closets with a trusted friend who can serve as your reality check. Some people actually have a disorder in which they can't part with anything. If this is you, please reach out for help.

5. **For every item you buy, make sure the same number of**

items are donated or sold. This is just another instance in which less is more. Have you ever walked into a cluttered room and felt like you were suffocating? You can feel this way in a stuffed closet as well.

6. Loretta Wilger-Asmus, owner of Looks Image Consulting in Naperville, is my "style on a budget" expert. Her advice is: **know your colors.** Everyone has certain colors that fit their hair color or skin tone. Buy clothes in these colors and make sure they work together so you can have just a few pieces to wear in different combinations. Her other advice is to always buy quality items, which last longer, preferably on sale. Loretta's exception to this rule is that you don't have to worry too much about quality if you're buying trendy items that will go out of style too fast for you to wear them out.

7. **When buying children's clothes,** you may want to listen to my friend Mary Kay, who once told me to make sure that I bought things that were the right size. Many parents buy things a little too big, thinking their kids can wear them longer. One mother I knew prided herself on saving a fortune by buying clothes for her twin boys at the end of season sales, figuring that if she bought clothes or shoes a size too big her boys would be able to wear them at a later date. Inevitably the boys' growth rate didn't correspond to the manufacturer's projection, and the clothes were too small before they even had a chance to wear them. What a waste.

Of course, there was an instance where I ignored Mary Kay's advice when buying a winter coat for KC. I bought a larger size for her but paid more for much higher quality and the coat made it through three seasons. We had to turn up the cuffs a bit during the first winter. The second winter it fit just right, and the last winter it was a little small, but she liked it so much she wore it all winter.

8. **Find alternative places to shop.** Discount chains like TJ Maxx and Marshalls offer designer clothes at far lower prices than the department stores. You can often save money shopping at high quality consignment shops and even make some money bringing them clothes you no longer wear. Somebody's castoff can be your perfect bargain and recycling clothes helps the environment.

9. **Keep your receipts with your purchases.** How many times have you brought something home and decided it wasn't quite right. It's very Wealth Watchers to be disciplined about what clothes you keep and what you return. I don't like to try things on in stores so I wind up trying them on at home and returning them if they don't fit. Even if you're good about trying on clothes in the store, I recommend keeping your purchase with the receipt in the shopping bag until you're sure you don't want to return or exchange it. Make sure you know the store's return policy before you buy. Maybe within a few days you'll find that you didn't really need your purchase after all. I come from a large family with seven children, and my mother had to constantly look for alternatives to buying new clothes for us. But I wonder if her frugality wound up backfiring as we all got older. All the girls in my family have overspent on clothing both for ourselves and for our kids. Maybe if you wear one too many hand-me-downs you just crack at some point and go overboard on new clothes. Looking back on it, I just should have been thankful for what we had. Many women shop according to unconscious patterns much as they eat according to such patterns. While I am no stranger to the shopping gene, I know that the daily discipline of Wealth Watchers can conquer these mysterious cravings.

> Love what you have, including yourself. Do you
> really need a new car, boat, dress, luxury vacation
> to make you happy? Wouldn't financial security
> be a more potent path to happiness?

My own family has gotten better at only buying what we need. I used to take KC shopping as an fun outing. Now we try to limit our clothes buying to one bout of trips for back-to-school shopping each year. KC was just diagnosed with scoliosis and has to wear a big brace; she needed new clothes to fit over the brace, so that became an exception to the rule. Some of our local schools have "clothing exchanges" where people bring used clothes to sell as part of a fundraiser for the school. People get back 60 percent of the proceeds for the sale of their items and the school keeps 40 percent. I know people who are big fans of shopping at Goodwill and other resale shops. And some friends have had great luck buying used clothing on the Internet through sites like Craigslist.

Dry Cleaning

Wealth Watchers Principle: Dry cleaning is an expense that is also an investment. It's important to take good care of your clothes so you don't have to replace them frequently.

For us, dry cleaning is a constant necessity, but I don't include it as a fixed or semi-fixed expense. I just pay for our dry cleaning from our DDI (daily disposable income). Our monthly dry cleaning bill, at its peak, was around $100. In order to cut back, I've started wearing shirts that can be machine washed more than blouses that need to be dry-cleaned. Dan has started wearing his machine washable Wheaton North coaching shirts instead of dress shirts. I'll also occasionally offer to take in Eddie's dry cleaning along with ours. I know I should let him handle his own expenses, but that's the mother in me trying to help him out—especially after I heard that he put one of his suits through the washer and dryer to save money on dry cleaning. He had no idea that it would ruin his suit. Still, it was kind of nice to hear that he was trying to save money.

BIG TICKET ITEMS PURCHASED INFREQUENTLY

Furniture/Home Appliances

Wealth Watchers Approach: Credit cards are indispensable for certain purchases, unless you are comfortable carrying around wads of hundred-dollar bills when shopping for big ticket items. How you pay off the monthly charges is another conversation. There are benefits to using credit cards, such as reward programs, friend and family discounts, and great discounts for opening accounts with specific retailers. But how many credit cards should you have at your disposal? Wouldn't life be easier if we used just one credit card, keeping another card on hand in case of an emergency or in case the first card was lost?

Household expenses are the ultimate miscellaneous category in any budget. If you are lucky, nothing will ever break and you will love all your home furnishings forever. Of course, if you are like me, Murphy's law will make sure that whatever can break will break and that those leaking washing machines and wheezing refrigerators will be expensive to repair or replace.

Household expenses also include such things as paying a plumber when the pipes freeze and burst, or an electrician to fix faulty wiring, or installing a new roof. These expenditures, usually unexpected and unplanned for, can become absolute budget breakers. Shopping for furniture is another tricky expenditure. If you shop at discount outlets, you might end up having to replace cheaply made merchandise. There are many ways to acquire high-quality furniture less expensively: estate sales, garage sales, Craigslist, cast-offs from family members. So before you shop, always ask yourself if it's possible to get what you really want for less money.

Smart Wealth Watchers know how much they can afford and when they can best afford it. If you take advantage of a store's zero-percent-interest promotion, make sure you pay the item off at least a month in advance of the date interest begins to accrue. I've heard horror stories of people not understanding when the final payment is due and being hit with a much higher interest rate. Ugh! If you do have to carry the cost of an item on a credit card, do your best to pay it off as soon as you can!

Because I'm a big believer in the Boy Scout motto—Be prepared—we automatically transfer a certain amount of money into our savings account each month. It's our emergency fund, but if we don't need to spend it that way, we use it for vacations. An unexpected expense might mean forgoing a summer trip. When our washing machine broke down one summer the cost to replace it was more than we had in our savings account. I spent a few weeks taking laundry to my mother's home because I so wanted to avoid buying new appliances with a credit card. Finally I cracked, and we did use our card for a new washing machine.

But remember, using credit cards can be a slippery slope. Let me be my own object lesson here. Something about buying that appliance seemed to open the flood gates. As long as we were blowing our budget, why not buy fresh towels? And we might as well replace Andy's and KC's well-worn bedspreads. Oh, and let's have the deck stained while we're at it since we really shouldn't put it off for another year. So what if we don't take a summer vacation. There's always next year.

Believe me, I know I don't sound like the wisest financial thinker. The truth is that my brain injury, which led me to create Wealth Watchers, continues to have a profound impact on our financial lives.

Before the brain injury I was actually making more money than Dan. Since the brain injury I've lost about 75 percent of my income. I look fine and I seem fine but I still struggle every day. I can't work at my old pace and we've had to add another person to our support staff to cover some of the work I would have done myself. A large percentage of brain injured people declare bankruptcy, but the Wealth Watchers regimen has kept us afloat. Before the brain injury, replacing a broken washer wouldn't have been a big deal. But now I'm aware that we have to work to set aside money for this kind of unexpected expense. The lesson: We can spend more money than we have when we're using credit cards . . . but we shouldn't. Even though we love to travel, we chose to forgo the summer vacation the year we bought the new washer, to cut down on massive credit card debt.

Vacation/Travel

Wealth Watchers Approach: *Know how much your vacation will cost and do your best to set aside the entire amount before you go.*

> Some of the best things in life really are free.
> Check your Community Events calendar for free
> or inexpensive entertainment in your area.

One of the most important things I've learned from *Wealth Watchers* is to set aside money every month for vacations. In my life, and probably yours too, family vacations are, like the credit card commercial says, priceless. Perhaps we've made a mistake using our vacation fund as our emergency fund; if something happens, what we lose is something valuable. But it does motivate me to save more money whenever possible.

In tough economic times, you may discover that there are many ways to take a vacation. You don't have to buy expensive plane tickets to pricey resorts in tropical locales to have fun. Vacations are the ultimate "discretionary" expenditure and you have to be certain you are not overspending on something now that you'll regret when the credit card bills arrive later. In the height of a recession, travel companies and the airlines offer amazing discounts on vacation packages. Of course, if you scale back even further, you can find ways to create memories closer to home. It's often much more about who you're with than where you're going that determines the success of a family vacation.

I never took a luxury trip as a child, but even though money was tight growing up, my parents would take us on road trips to Florida almost every spring break. It was such a big deal to stay in a hotel room that not one of the nine of us minded piling into one room. The younger children slept on the floor in sleeping bags, and it felt like camping indoors. Mom was big on packing a cooler with sandwiches and we usually had cereal in our hotel room before heading out for another day on the road. I've inherited my mom's frugal travel gene. I'm always figuring out ways to take a great trip without breaking the bank. In August of 2007, for example, we were able to take a fabulous and relatively inexpensive vacation to Germany. This is where my large, strategically located family really pays off. My brother Larry and his wife Susi live on Insel Reichenau, a German island that's located just across the border from Switzerland. Susi's family is from Insel Reichenau and we were lucky enough to have Larry marry into her family. It not only gave us a free place to stay, it gave us the benefit of knowing local people who generously showed us the sights and served us the local food. We also stayed with my sister Gay, who lives in Berlin. Sure, most people don't have family in exotic destinations but there are so many inexpensive ways to enjoy traveling—from youth hostels to elder hostels to volunteer/tourism opportunities to apartment swaps with people in foreign cities—that you shouldn't just assume wonderful travel experiences are out of reach.

Of course, our "free" vacation wasn't really free. Though we used miles to buy our round-trip airplane tickets, I had to purchase some miles for one of our tickets. This, plus ticketing fees cost nearly $330. We also had to buy airplane tickets from Zurich to Berlin but that was less than $300. And there were some unusual ancillary costs, like the new underwear I had to buy because I knew we'd have to hang our laundry outside to dry when we stayed with my relatives. There are still more things that one really doesn't think about when budgeting for a trip, like gifts for our hosts—and souvenirs to bring home. The final cost of our "free trip" was close to $1,500—but it was also priceless.

ENTERTAINMENT

Holiday Celebrations

Wealth Watchers Principle: Many hands make light work . . . and a less expensive party.

Celebrations don't have to break the bank. I know some cultures put an immense amount of pressure on families to do things a certain way during specific holidays. And in these instances I'm sure there's a certain amount of pride involved. But what we really need to do is to take a deep look inside our hearts and our bank accounts to be sure that we're making the best possible choice. No one should put themselves or their families into debt just to fund a celebration. There are so many ways to make an occasion joyful without spending huge amounts of money. Value is in the eye of the beholder, but it just seems to me like a mistake to go into debt for a party. The Wealth Watchers philosophy would be to find a less expensive alternative to what might otherwise be a very expensive day.

Celebrations are certainly a big deal in my family. We have a long history of throwing great parties. In fact, my grandparents had a toga party years before *Animal House.* They were invited to the premiere of *Cleopatra* in Chicago, so to commemorate the event they held a party where everyone wore wonderful costumes. I love looking at the old family pictures and seeing my grandfather, a judge on the U.S. Court of Appeals for the Seventh Circuit, along with my great aunts Alice and Florence, all wearing togas. But the truth, as my mother tells me, was that the parties cost very little. Their secret was to have a theme, stay focused on a reasonable amount of food and drink, and just invite people they really liked.

I was impressed, recently, when I went to a friend's home for a high school graduation party and saw how much fun the twenty or so guests were having despite the very simple spread. My friend told me that he and his wife went to Costco and bought hamburgers and hot dogs in bulk—five dozen of each, along with buns and rolls and a few supersized containers of potato salad and cole slaw. They bought family packs of chips, several big jars of salsa, and several massive packs of cookies. They also bought bulk packages of paper plates, napkins, plastic utensils and cups. The whole thing cost less than $150. Assorted two-liter bottles of soda and beer came to another $50. My friend's wife baked a graduation cake using approximately $6 worth of ingredients. My friend manned the backyard barbeque to keep the hot food coming, and the son extended an open invitation to friends who came and went all afternoon and into the night. For around $200, they had a great party, no one went hungry, and they created wonderful memories for themselves and their son.

If you've recently given a party then you're well aware of the potential expense involved. But with the recession, more people are having inexpensive potluck dinners at home rather than gathering at restaurants or bars where the tab is always more than you expect. As the economy rebounds, people will undoubtedly start going out again, but they hopefully will give the potluck a permanent spot in their entertainment plans.

Our family holiday celebrations tend to be potlucks, and we are usually told what to bring. It's no secret that I'm the worst cook in the family. Once I was asked to bring canned peas to a family Thanksgiving celebration, and instead of being humiliated I was relieved. Canned peas are right up my alley. No matter who brings what, though, everyone enjoys the variety of fare and nobody bears the entire cost of a party.

Weddings/Graduations/Other Milestones

Wealth Watchers Approach: *You don't have to have an expensive wedding to create the memory of a lifetime.*

I just love weddings. I love the dresses. I love the decorations. I love the whole celebration. And I have to admit, I love over-the-top, outrageously expensive, obscenely ostentatious weddings. My Aunt Jean says that there's no such thing as "too much" when it comes to someone's Christmas decorations. I feel the same way about weddings.

But my practical side thinks it's insane to go into debt for a party. I actually have no problem with eloping—as long as your families don't disown you! For many people, however, wedding memories aren't complete without family and friends. Beyond that, it takes a very mature person to understand the difference between a marriage and a wedding. And it takes a very mature person to be able to understand the financial impact of an expensive wedding. Money is the number one cause of divorce in our country. Why would anyone want to start out their married life by going into debt for a party that's over in a day?

But Wealth Watchers is never meant to be judgmental. We're just here to help you think before you spend. If you have your heart set on a huge wedding, then go for it. But you'll likely save lots of heartache if you save up for the entire cost before the big day. I know of one young woman and her fiancé who have spent the past year saving up for their wedding. They are paying for almost everything themselves and the wedding will ultimately cost close to $35,000. Even though they've chosen to have a fancy wedding, I have the feeling that this couple will be financially stable. They've been able to set a financial goal and delay getting married until they reach that goal. Maybe their next goal will be to own a home and pay it off as quickly as possible.

Every family is different: I know of weddings in which the groom's family pays for the bar at the reception. And in some cases, families split the entire cost of the wedding. And of course the bride and groom sometimes pay for the wedding themselves. I think the days of the bride's family paying for the whole wedding by default are at their end.

When Dan and I were married there was a big part of me that felt very uncomfortable with the idea of a big wedding because I had been married before. It was difficult for me to ask my family and friends to watch me get married once again. But Dan had never been married and our marriage was something I wanted to celebrate. So we decided on a picnic in my mom's backyard and invited nearly three hundred people.

I also felt uncomfortable with the idea of wearing a wedding dress but I found what I thought was the perfect outfit, on sale! I bought a beautiful white blouse from Neiman Marcus and white palazzo pants from another store: The entire outfit cost less than $200 including shoes and jewelry. Unfortunately, I didn't put the outfit together until the morning of our wedding. When I looked in the mirror, I started laughing so hard I began to cry. It looked like Elvis Presley's famous Vegas jumpsuit. Dan only made fun of me a little bit.

Judge Bauer, a close family friend, performed such a nice ceremony. Eddie and Andy were about four and nine years old at the time so we made it a very kid friendly wedding. We had pony rides and a Good Humor ice cream cart. Our menu included White Castle hamburgers and Brown's Chicken and champagne. We had a wading pool filled with ice and bottled beer and soft drinks. The only big expense was the invitations. My cousin

Mary Sue once told me that an invitation sets the tone for a party. Because our wedding was on the Fourth of July, she found invitations that had a blue sparkled background with red foil trim. They were nearly $5 each but they were just perfect. Value is in the eye of the beholder. Even with those three hundred guests, the entire wedding cost us less than $5,000.

Social Expenses and Gifts for Friends/Family

Wealth Watchers Approach: Being thoughtful beats overspending.

My cousin Mary Lou Wehrli and her husband Herb Nadelhoffer shared a great lesson at one of our Wealth Watchers meetings. Between them, they have so many nieces and nephews that they decided that rather than give each one a birthday gift every year, they take each one on an outing to some special place. I love that. An experience without clutter. A memory that can last forever instead of an object or toy that can't last.

With money, as with everything else, less is usually more. Not every family can afford to give a Nintendo Wii as a birthday gift, but there are ways to express your love without breaking your bank account. Lately I've been turning away from giving "stuff." Most kids, including mine, have way more things than

> The best gifts come from the heart.
> Being thoughtful doesn't have to be expensive.

they can appreciate and use, and I hate to add to anyone's household clutter.

It would be great to set aside a certain amount of money each month for gifts, but in this economy it is a luxury I cannot afford. Banks used to promote "Christmas Club" accounts for people to set aside money each month so that they could afford to buy gifts when the holidays rolled around. I used to think they were kind of hokey but now I see their value.

I've definitely become a much more thoughtful gift giver because of Wealth Watchers. We still pay for gifts from our DDI (daily disposable income), so when we spend money on a gift, we have that much less to use on ourselves. It brings a small sense of sacrifice to the enterprise which adds meaning to the gift giving. Since I'm not so quick to part with money anymore, I'm more careful about the amount of money that I spend. But I'm also more careful about choosing something that someone would really like.

Dining Out with Friends and Family

Wealth Watchers Approach: Being a Wealth Watcher doesn't mean that you never have any fun.

We always look forward to going out with our friends but it's not something that we do every weekend. It's just too expensive. Instead we've made an effort to visit each other at home, with everyone contributing food and drink. As a family we've cut back on our restaurant bills by ordering water instead of buying drinks. The cost of alcohol can easily exceed the cost of the entire meal. Even taking a pass on a soft drink can really cut down on a restaurant bill. Try skipping the drink or appetizer and see how much that small step allows you to save in a year.

We tend to save between $10 and $20 dollars per restaurant bill just by cutting out soft drinks.

Our objective at Wealth Watchers isn't simply to save and scrimp for every dime but to find a balance between enjoying life and saving enough money to be secure.

Since dining out is one of the largest discretionary expenses for most people, it's worth taking a hard look at what our eating-out habits cost us. Eating out for either lunch or dinner is a joy and a treat for us social animals. But it's not cheap.

About five years ago, I read a great article by Carolyn Bigda, a business reporter for the Chicago Tribune. She decided to do an experiment to figure out what she was spending to eat lunch and dinner out rather than cooking for herself at home. Her findings were eye-opening. She asked: "Would more homemade meals during the work week lower the total food bill?"

Here's a detailed look at what she discovered:

Eating Out

Breakfast:

Five days a week: $3.04 per day for

Coffee	$1.79
Banana	$0.25
Muffin	$1.00
Five-day total:	**$15.20**

Lunch:

Monday	Tuna sandwich with pickle	$4.00
Tuesday	Panini, pickles, and bag of chips	$6.46
Wednesday	Fish fillet and small salad	$4.96
Thursday	Soup and baguette	$4.22
Friday	Large salad with bread	$7.88
Total:		**$27.52**

Dinner:

Monday	Vegetable lo mein and egg roll	$11.00, with tip
Tuesday	Salad (with chicken) and bread	$8.35
Wednesday	Chicken schwarma sandwich	$4.00
Thursday	Sweet and sour chicken entree	$13.00, with tip
Friday	Two slices of cheese pizza	$4.00
Total:		**$40.35**

Five-day total:	**$83.07**

Eating In

Breakfast:

Five days a week: $1.39 per day

Coffee	$0.26
Orange juice	$0.30
Cereal (with milk)	$0.83
Five-day total:	**$6.95**

Lunch:

Five days a week: $3.01 per day for turkey pita sandwich (with lettuce and mustard), yogurt, crackers, and orange

Pita bread	$0.16
Lettuce	$0.20
Deli turkey	$0.52
Yogurt	$0.89
Crackers	$0.74
Orange	$0.50
Five-day total:	**$15.05**

Dinner:

Monday—Progresso vegetable soup ($2.89), roll with butter ($0.60)	$3.49
Tuesday—Broiled steak ($4.50), broccoli ($0.32), and egg noodles with butter ($0.43)	$5.25
Wednesday—Salmon fillet with onion ($3.15), baked potato with butter ($0.60), broccoli ($0.32)	$4.07
Thursday—Baked eggplant with marinara sauce and mozzarella cheese	$2.92
Friday—Rotini pasta with marinara sauce ($1.00), salad with lettuce, cucumber, tomatoes, and dressing ($1.41)	$2.41
Total:	**$18.14**
Five-day total:	**$40.14**

A close look at what Carolyn ate shows she was not being extravagant, either eating out or at home. She did her experiment in 2005 so food prices were not markedly different than today. Eating out was more than 50 percent more expensive than making food for herself at home. In her research, Carolyn also discovered that the average person age twenty-four or younger spends 8 percent of his or her salary on food prepared outside of the home. That is the highest of all age groups even though young workers on average draw the lowest income.

The experiment in eating at home certainly proved that it is the far cheaper alternative. But I liked Carolyn's suggestion that a balance of eating out and at home is the best solution. Wealth Watchers believe that the best solution is one that takes a high quality of life into account.

Lunch with Colleagues

Wealth Watchers Approach: *You can save a lot of money by bringing your own lunch just several days a week.*

Obviously, eating out is expensive. I hear from so many people, especially young people, that eating in restaurants is their biggest financial black hole. I was recently with a group of twenty-five women chatting about where we waste the most money. Nearly everyone in the room went out for lunch every day, and spent $7 to $10 per day!

Do you really mean to be spending over $2,000 a year just for lunch? If not, then what are you doing about it? We all have barriers to handling our money better. Maybe the barrier is just remembering to pick up groceries to make your own lunch at home. You don't have to make your lunch every day. Just a few days a week will make a difference. Maybe Wednesday should be the day you treat yourself by going out to lunch. Wealth Watchers isn't about *never* going out for lunch or *always* going out to lunch. It's an attempt to spend money with awareness.

All of these ideas may seem so obvious, but I think many of us have drifted away from some very basic ideals. We forget that the best way to get ahead is to proceed slowly and steadily. I've said throughout this book that the route to financial stability is a search for balance and an effort to make smart choices. You find balance by examining carefully how you spend your money. When you think about going out to lunch with colleagues, don't rush to join the group and then drop $15 or $20 just because everyone else does it. Make eating out an occasional thing and try to have lunch only with those colleagues whose company you really enjoy. In other words, use your Wealth Watchers experience to evaluate not just what you are spending but what that spending will buy you. The discipline of saving money will begin to have a profound impact on the quality of your experiences. In that way, you will be reaching for the kwan.

THE WISH LIST

Wealth Watchers Approach: *You can have almost anything you want as long as you set aside the money ahead of time. Be mindful of how much little luxuries are costing you over the course of a year. You may be able to give them up more easily than you think, allowing you to save more money to buy what you truly desire.*

At one of our early Wealth Watchers meetings, a woman shared with the group that she had bought a coveted pair of gorgeous Italian leather shoes. Before she discovered Wealth Watchers, she would have simply used her credit card. Instead, she saved up by cutting little expenses, such as eating out, until she could afford to pay cash for the shoes. It only took her a couple of weeks and she felt far better being able to pay cash than she would have charging those shoes to a credit card.

Why does anyone do anything if it's not to reach a goal? The idea behind Wealth Watchers is that you can have just about anything you want. You just need to plan for it. The first goal of Wealth Watchers is to spend less money than you make. The next goal is to avoid buying "things" that you don't need.

Every once in a while, a special meeting or presentation will tempt me to buy a new outfit for work. I've just had to remind myself to go through my closet to make sure that I really need something. And the truth is, I usually don't.

I also have a goal when it comes to my children and money. I'm really hoping that they will all make good choices about spending and saving. I'll know I've done a good job if they don't ask us for money when they're adults.

One of my biggest goals has been to own our home outright. Before the brain injury we were actually only a few years away from being mortgage free. Now that goal is going to take longer to reach, but it's still my goal.

My other goal is not so much for myself or my family. It's about helping other people set and track a daily goal for spending and saving so that we are all better able to handle a financial setback. The sad truth is that our country isn't doing much better than we are individually. Collectively and individually we spend more money than we make, and that is just not OK. We'll all feel better about the financial world when the personal savings rates are back up around 10 percent again (as they often were from the 1960s through the 1980s) and our bankruptcy and foreclosure rates reach an all-time low. That is a worthwhile goal for everyone.

CHAPTER SIX

A Call to Action

Money is a terrible master but an excellent servant.
P. T. Barnum

My path to Wealth Watchers has been both very painful and incredibly rewarding. I've learned enough along the way to be able to connect the financial dots that we generally miss. If I hadn't suffered a brain injury and walked a mile in the shoes of people who have made financial mistakes, I wouldn't be where I am today.

Thanks to my huge and caring family and all of our friends, I'm able to look at things from many different perspectives. I grew tired of making mistakes that caused financial problems. I would never want to live through the consequences again. But I've also been exhilarated by the effort to get my financial house in order.

I've had the privilege to spend a great deal of time in Washington, DC, talking to legislators, people at the Federal Reserve, politicians, and lobbyists about what is being done or not being done at a national level. From these conversations, I have come to believe that the way forward is through education. I've learned so much from our grass-roots effort to promote financial literacy through Wealth Watchers and I've come away even more convinced that we must be our own best advocates when it comes to financial stability.

> No "thing" feels as good as money in the bank.
> There's something very uncomfortable about debt
> and there's something very comforting
> about money in the bank.

Wealth Watchers is really about education and discipline, about learning and doing. As a nation, we have to place greater urgency on financial literacy, so as individuals we can understand the basic principles of how the system works and how we can successfully manage our money. We have to be wiser about not getting into debt and falling prey to the machinations of financial institutions that know how to manipulate the system—and our wallets—better than we do. But education must come first; without it we inevitably get into trouble and lose our way financially. Life can be tough enough but when you add money woes to the general burden, the results can be devastating.

We forget that as bad as financial troubles are today, they used to be far worse. People have been struggling with debt since the earliest days of trade and commerce. A *New Yorker* article in the spring of 2009 noted that under ancient Roman law, it was common for a debtor to end up as a slave. For centuries, debtors' prisons abounded in Europe, filled with desperate people who often died there owing only tiny sums. Debtors were not given prison terms like actual criminals. They stayed until they or their family figured out how to repay their debt. The American colonies were settled by, among others, debtors who had been expelled from their European homelands. And there were debtors' prisons in the United States until the early nineteenth century.

Fortunately, we abolished the barbaric treatment of the indebted. As the advent of bankruptcy laws created a novel way to look at an old problem, being in debt took on a new meaning in our country. Though declaring bankruptcy was a source of shame, it was no longer life threatening. In 1946, just 8,600 Americans filed for bankruptcy, the number in 2008 surpassed one million, and there will be many more as the economic crisis continues. In my view, merely confronting bad debt treats only the symptom, not the problem. The bigger challenge is to teach people to avoid financial problems in the first place.

FINANCIAL LITERACY

Charles Schwab, famed investment guru and founder of Charles Schwab Investments Services, said, "While there are many causes to the economic problems facing the country, it is undeniable that a lack of financial literacy is a contributing factor." Amen to that.

One thing I've learned through my Wealth Watchers work is that it doesn't matter how smart or rich or old you are, money troubles cross all boundaries and layers of society. Reading about the wealthy clients who lost everything in the Bernard Madoff scandal makes it clear that a financial crisis can arise for unexpected victims in unexpected ways. The challenge of successfully handling money transcends education, income level, IQ, and age. But the good news is that just as anyone is potentially vulnerable, anyone can also take steps to avoid being a victim.

The current housing crisis illustrates the dangers of an inadequate financial education. As I noted earlier, far too many of us simply ignored the 28/36 rule about how much income people should devote to their monthly mortgage. Instead of sticking to a mortgage payment that was 28 percent of pretax income, it became commonplace to take on loans as high as 50 percent, with the expectation that housing prices would rise forever. Whether it was ignorance or arrogance, the results were the same.

The standard way to buy a home in the good old days was with a thirty-year fixed rate mortgage with 20 percent down. People had to rent or live with their families until they could save enough money for a down payment to buy their first home. They weren't enticed into tapping into their home equity to buy a boat or a vacation home. Who would have thought that one day lenders would let people buy homes with no down payment or without even verifying their income? Who knew that lenders would throw credit at people, with little or no regard to their ability to repay the loan?

We have to admit it, we are a society that has grown to expect instant gratification. It is this tendency unchecked by financial literacy that has contributed the most to our economic woes.

The Great Depression was a defining moment for an entire generation. Its survivors never thought about money in the same way again. The people all around me have been touched in a very personal way by the scope of the devastating economic downturn that started in late 2007, gathered steam in September 2008, and has yet to reach a conclusion. But I am an eternal optimist. If an increased interest in financial literacy emerges from the rubble of foreclosures and bankruptcies, this crisis will have been the catalyst for invaluable learning. Wouldn't it be great to have our next generation known as a Generation of Savers?

We do know that this downturn had deep roots—banking deregulation, the subprime mortgage disaster, the credit crisis—but if we analyze this at a personal level, we see that it was mainly about uneducated borrowers and bad financial habits. So many Americans don't understand the mechanics of debt or the greater rules that guide our financial system, and there is rarely a cushion to soften the blow.

It's very telling that the states with the most foreclosures in 2008 were those in which people put the highest percentage of their income toward their mortgages. Why are foreclosure rates at an all time high? Because most of us had never heard of the 28/36 rule. Those of us who got in over our heads probably had no sense of how reckless it was to take on this much debt until we had a personal setback.

The "Greatest Generation" paid cash for almost everything, other than their home. There was a long period of time after the Great Depression when the personal savings rate in our country was around 9 percent. In the 1970s, it was often above 14 percent. People actually had a cushion in case they faced an unexpected job loss or a prolonged illness. And then something changed.

Older parents who came of age in this post-Depression period never would have taught their children about credit cards or questionable mortgage products because they'd never encountered such easy access to credit.

CREDIT CARDS

The first credit cards appeared in the 1950s, and bank-sponsored cards became popular in the 1960s. When banks began to see how lucrative easy access to credit could be, they flooded the marketplace with an increasing number of loan products. Over time, consumer debt skyrocketed while our personal savings rate plummeted but people grew comfortable living in debt. It was this "everyone else is doing it" new norm that got us into trouble. This is where Wealth Watchers comes in. If you know how much money you can spend each day, without going into debt, if you understand that every day and every dollar really do count, you can avoid a life of debt or at least have a plan of action for getting out of debt. This kind of simple financial literacy is crucial to finding financial peace of mind. No matter how many people I meet through Wealth Watchers, I am constantly amazed by their stories. There doesn't seem to be any obstacle that can't be overcome with just a little knowledge and discipline.

Natalie is a sixty-six-year-old grandmother who attended a series of Wealth Watchers meetings with me. She told me that she had once been a single mother on welfare raising four children. In order to get by, Natalie used her credit card (which she'd obtained before she went on welfare). But she was soon using it more often than was realistic or necessary.

"I was spending money on things I really didn't need or have the money to buy," she recalls. "I was living beyond my means. I'd buy things for the house, clothes, and soon the credit card bills got out of control."

Eventually, Natalie knew she had to stop herself so she took a unique step. "I locked my credit card in the trunk of the car," she said. "When I'd go into a store, I'd have to ask myself, 'Do I really need this?' If it meant going back out to the car to get the credit card out of the trunk, I really had to think twice about what I was buying. It stopped me from purchasing things unwisely."

Fortunately, Natalie's life changed and her financial situation improved. But she recently embraced Wealth Watchers in order to maintain fiscal discipline. "I learned where I was wasting money," she said. "Even something like buying coffee every day when I could take a cup with me from home made a difference. The little things add up. I became more comfortable. Living within my means makes life easier."

Of course, Natalie was hardly alone with her credit card struggles. Credit card debt is nothing short of a national crisis. It's been obscured by the housing crisis and the Wall Street meltdown, but for many people, it is a serious and debilitating problem. In 2008, according to the Federal Reserve, the total outstanding credit card debt carried by Americans reached a record $951 billion! That's nearly a trillion dollars just in credit card debt! It is truly mind boggling. Credit card defaults were on track to reach 10 percent in 2009 which means that along with home foreclosures, a large number of Americans would be facing personal bankruptcy. In May 2009, the *New York Times* reported that the nation's nineteen largest banks could expect nearly $83 billion in credit card losses by the end of 2010. If unemployment continues to rise, that number could be far higher.

I understand how people get into credit card trouble. I've done it myself. Credit cards let us spend money even if we don't have any. As I pointed out earlier in the book, it's too easy to swipe that piece of plastic at the checkout counter and forget that you've just taken a loan that will need to be repaid . . . with interest. It's especially easy to reach for the credit card if you've lost your job and you need to buy food or pay for medicine. But this is a slippery slope. When you fail to pay your credit card bills on time, the banks will charge you ridiculously high interest rates, penalties, and fees that will sink you deeper into debt. Bankruptcy, the ultimate conclusion of this kind of debt, may resolve the short-term problem, but it creates the paradoxical new problem: your credit rating is now so damaged you may have trouble trying to borrow money again, for a house, for college, for a car, for anything. It's remarkable how many people, either inadvertently or thoughtlessly, have badly damaged or destroyed their credit scores. It's shocking to see the way financial institutions have leaped in to take advantage of those mistakes.

This is where financial literacy is so critical. The banks found a lucrative revenue stream by charging these late fees, cash advance fees, and any other kind of fee they could legally tack on. In 2007, banks collected more than $18 billion in penalties and fees! Ugh! In 2009, one major bank sent a warning to its customers that if they missed a single payment, the interest rate on their credit cards could jump to nearly 30 percent! How is that legal? And how many people actually read those ubiquitous notices sent out by the credit card issuers? We need to read the fine print and know what we're signing up for. In fairness to the credit card industry, no one made us buy things we couldn't afford . . . they just made it possible. President Obama has pushed hard for legislation that would force banks to eliminate unfair interest rates and fees. That is long overdue, but it isn't really enough. No matter how much legislation is enacted, people can still get into trouble with credit card debt, regardless of whether the interest rate is 15 percent or 30 percent.

The fact is, Americans don't understand debt, which is one reason they have too much of it. A 2009 survey conducted by the Harvard Business School and Dartmouth College asked 1,000 people how long it would take to pay off a hypothetical credit card debt by making the minimum payment. Only 36 percent of the respondents were able to figure out how many years it would take for the amount they owed on their credit cards to double. More than 18 percent had no answer and 32 percent overestimated the time period. The survey also revealed how little Americans understand compound interest and its impact on debt. Annamaria Lusardi, a professor of economics at Dartmouth said, "Even those with a college degree don't have an understanding of basic finance."

So what can we do? The philosopher George Santayana said, "Those who do not remember the past are doomed to repeat it."

Nowhere is that as true as in our personal financial lives. If we don't understand how we got into trouble, we'll not only have a painful time trying to get out of it, but we'll likely fall into the same traps again and again. Let's end this vicious cycle!

I'm probably one of the few people in the country who enjoys reading *The National Strategy for Financial Literacy*. This document is nothing less than a call to action. As a nation, we have to take drastically different measures to mend our collective financial condition. As things are now, every man, woman, and child in the United States would have to write a check for nearly $194,000 to eliminate our national debt. But maybe there's another way out of this hole . . . like increasing our personal savings rate so we're not living on the edge of disaster with only the federal government to bail us out.

We also need to push our governmental representatives to address the damage that deregulation has caused in the banking industry since 1980. The loosening or elimination of many long-held regulations set off a frenzy of profit making by opportunistic financial institutions that led directly to the current global economic meltdown. According to Gretchen Morgenson, a finance columnist for the *New York Times*, their transgressions are many and they've always hurt most the consumers who can least afford the pain.

She points out that lenders consistently find new ways to squeeze more profit from borrowers. Though prevailing interest rates have fallen to the low single digits in recent years, the rates credit issuers routinely charged even to borrowers with good credit records have risen to 19.1 percent in 2008 from 17.7 percent in 2005. This has added billions of dollars in interest charges annually to credit card bills.

Average late fees soared, from less than $13 in 1994 to $35 in 2007, and fees charged when customers exceed their credit limits more than doubled to $26 from $11 in that same time period. Banks find all sorts of remarkable fees to charge unsuspecting customers, according to Morgenson. Mortgage lenders tack on such fees as $75 email charges, $100 document preparation costs, and $70 courier fees—"bringing the average to $700 a mortgage, according to the Department of Housing and Urban Development," said Morgenson in a July 2008 column. Junk fees like these are up 50 percent in recent years, according to Michael A. Kratzer, president of FeeDisclosure.com, a site designed to help consumers reduce fees on mortgages.

What is the lesson here? Smart consumers ask a lot of questions, make sure they understand exactly what they are signing up for, and know immediately what to avoid when it comes to credit products.

If we don't start educating our children and young adults now, the problem will be compounded with each new generation. And therein lies my soapbox sermon: If adults can get themselves into such financial chaos, how in the world can our children hope to avoid financial turmoil if we don't offer them a solid financial education?

EDUCATING OUR KIDS

Financial literacy must become a national priority in the classroom, in the workplace, and in our communities. According to the federal government's 2006 report *National Strategy for Financial Literacy,* young Americans spend $150 billion each year. Yet they don't understand basic financial concepts such as annual percentage rates, inflation, and interest. A survey done in 2008 found that high school seniors correctly answered just 48 percent of personal finance and economic questions in a nationwide survey conducted by the Federal Reserve. It was the worst score

> A wise person once said, "Parents who give their kids everything, give their kids nothing." There's nothing wrong with telling our kids that "it's not in our budget." "No" can be one of the best things we tell our kids . . . and ourselves.

in the six surveys the Federal Reserve has conducted in this age group.

According to a 2009 Associated Press article, only three states—Utah, Missouri, and Tennessee—require high school students to take a one-semester personal finance class before graduating. Another seventeen states require finance skills to be covered in other subjects such as economics, social studies, or math. We are talking about just twenty out of the fifty United States, and these classes just scratch the surface. Sometimes you don't have to leave home to learn valuable financial lessons. My son Eddie, who is now in his mid twenties and worked two jobs while finishing his degree, recently struggled with financial issues very common for his age. It was a real awakening for me to realize that he had so little financial awareness. I'll let Eddie explain:

"I had very minimal financial knowledge as a high school and college student and even after graduating. I overdrew my account on numerous occasions and never seemed to learn from my mistakes. To this day, I am still struggling to handle my finances responsibly. I border on the inept when it comes to handling monthly finances such as rent and bill paying.

"All this made daily life extremely stressful. As a result of often being short on money to cover my rent and pay my bills at the end of the month, I had to resort to asking my parents for help. So here I was, badly wanting to be independent but inevitably needing assistance.

"When my mom introduced me to the Wealth Watchers concept, it made perfect sense. The basic principles are very clear: track what you spend and never spend more than you make. It is so simple yet so many people can't do it. For me, the daily discipline changed me enough so that I am no longer oblivious to what was a very serious problem. I'm not even close to being financially savvy but at least I'm informed."

You can't imagine how it hurts me to hear Eddie describe his own financial education this way. I know I could have and should have spent time teaching him about how to think about and handle money when he was a child, certainly as a teenager. So when I think about the need for financial literacy in this country, I don't have to go beyond my own front door. I'm determined to do better and to help give his generation a deeper and more balanced understanding of how to handle money.

Of course, this isn't easy. But it is simple. The best way—in fact, the only way—to resolve an economic crisis like ours is to take personal responsibility for your money by learning to manage it better. Wealth Watchers is simple. The methods are purposely not very complex because I wanted it to work for everyone, across generations. The key to success is self-discipline, the will to want to make a change and stick to the program until it has the intended impact.

I introduced the Wealth Watchers concept to a class called Personal Money Management for Spending and Saving at Benedictine University in Lisle, Illinois. The class was taught by Professor Vicki Jobst and she invited me to come and share some of the Wealth Watchers ideas. I was really pleased with the students' responses. Here are a few:

A freshman said, "The first lesson that I learned about managing my money is to write down all of my purchases. Before, I really didn't think this method would work because I thought I could just keep track of my money in my head. After writing down all of my purchases I really found out where all my money was going. By realizing where all my money was going, I found out that I spent a lot of my money on unnecessary purchases like fast food. Now when I keep track of my money, I always think before I purchase."

A junior had this to say: "Before taking this course, I considered myself a spender, now I feel like I have converted myself to a person who is smart and conscious about what I spend my money on. Just by posting in my Wealth Watchers journal, I cut my spending down from $100 a week to about $50 a week."

A senior added, "An important lesson I learned is to plan ahead and begin saving for any major expenses. I would always rely on my credit card for any major purchases. I had all my money in a CD so I didn't have access to it. So I used my credit card to buy things and I ended up spending more to do that. Because the interest and fees on my credit card are higher than the interest earned on the money kept in the CDs. I decided to leave some money in a savings account instead of putting it all in a CD. Now when I need money I don't have to use my credit card."

My hope is that these financial lessons will stay with them throughout their lives. It's amazing that we insist our children learn spelling, math, science, grammar, and history but don't insist on teaching the critical life skill of finance.

In an Associated Press newspaper article,
I found these excellent tips for teaching children
how to handle money. They were supplied by
the Indiana Youth Institute (www.iyi.org).

AGES 4–7

—Assign real or play money values to tasks or extra chores. Children can later use the money for rewards like staying up ten minutes later or a movie night with popcorn.
—Set aside a decorated container to save money for purchases.

AGES 8–12

—Talk about different saving options and accounts that pay interest.
—While grocery shopping, compare prices among brands and have children practice estimating what the total bill will be.
—Help children create an imaginary bank account where they can receive income and pay costs while recording the money going in and out of the account. Review the balance at the end of each month.

AGES 13 AND UP

—Create a budget as if teens were living on their own and talk about summer job options.

—Once teens begin working, help them open a checking and savings account so they learn to use the accounts.

—Discuss the importance of having good credit and how to get it.

—Visit car dealership web sites to show teens how to estimate payments, maintenance expenses, and gas costs for various vehicles.

—Discuss the difference between wants and needs.

The Money Savvy Generation at msgen.com is also a great resource for teaching children about money.

ENLIGHTENED SELF-INTEREST AND OTHER SIGNS OF HOPE

Visa, McDonald's, and the Value of Wealth Watchers

One of the positive outcomes of the economic crisis has been the emergence of financial education advocacy groups from both the public and private sectors. Given the vast need and long neglect of this issue, there is much to be done. But we have to start somewhere.

I've always loved bringing people together for a cause. I think of myself as one of those connectors that Malcolm Gladwell described in *The Tipping Point*. My passion about financial literacy is the engine behind Wealth Watchers. It drives me crazy that so many people in America are in bad financial straits simply because they never learned the basics of handling money. So I decided to do something about it. One of my favorite quotes comes from Margaret Mead. She said, *"Never doubt that a small group of thoughtful, committed citizens can change the world. Indeed, it is the only thing that ever has."* On my crusade for financial literacy, I have met thoughtful, committed people who think and feel the way I do, and I've realized that it might in fact only take one determined person within an organization to make things happen.

Not long ago, for example, I was introduced to Jason Alderman, a very determined young man who runs the financial literacy programs for Visa, USA. As director of financial education for Visa, Jason spends his time setting up programs and doing surveys about financial literacy. Visa has been doing this for more than a decade.

At first blush, it seems ironic that a credit card company would be the catalyst for financial education, given how much financial trouble credit cards have caused. But many people don't understand what Visa does. Though the Visa name appears on credit cards, Visa actually provides the network that processes credit card transactions. Visa works with the banks that use its network and brand. But it is the individual banks that set the interest rates and fees, collect payments, and profit from the credit they offer through the cards. In fact, Visa has taken a strong interest in educating the public about all things financial.

When I met Jason, I had been talking to McDonald's about using the Wealth Watchers programs for its employees. They were interested and I thought it might be a good idea to bring in Visa as a partner. So matchmaker that I am, I introduced Jason to the folks at McDonald's human resources department. In a relatively short time, McDonald's launched its financial literacy program incorporating our Wealth Watchers journals with Visa's Practical Money Skills for Life program To date, they've handed out 500,000 Wealth Watchers journals to McDonald's employees around the country.

For Visa and Jason, the goal is to reach as many people as possible in need of a financial education. This is my goal too. I'm hoping that you are getting excited about the prospect of joining what promises to be a national movement.

Jason is one of the most knowledgeable people I've met when it comes to the financial issues people struggle with. Here are some of his thoughts:

"We see three key pillars to our efforts: budgeting, saving, and the wise use of credit. These are the areas with the biggest need.

"First, **budgeting** is like using your seatbelt or flossing your teeth. Everybody knows you should do it and most do it occasionally. But we need to do it more and it doesn't matter if you have $100 or $1 million. If you don't have a plan and understand where the money comes from and where it is going, you are in trouble.

"We started a program with players in the National Football League called Financial Football. What I've heard from these guys is that you have to have a budget. And they have seen the horror stories. Players sign the big contract, then spend more than they have, buy the Bentleys, the mansions, and then they break their leg, the career ends, no more money is coming in and they have enormous debts they cannot pay and a lifestyle they can't support.

"Second, we need to **save**. Since the recession started, we have gone from a negative savings rate back to a positive one. It's a reflex reaction but as a nation, we do need to save more. A lot of the troubles people are having today could be mitigated with more savings. The rule of thumb is to have six months worth of mortgage payments saved. It's important to understand the virtues of saving.

"Third, we also have to focus on **the wise use of credit.** We look at all forms of loans and help people understand the ramifications of taking out a loan. A credit card is a loan product. You may choose to pay back the balance every month, but it is still a loan. You have to understand the long-term impact of buying over time. If you pay over time, will you pay more than if you hadn't financed the purchase? We don't try to talk people out of loan products but we want them to understand whether to and how to take out a loan.

"I find common ground with Wealth Watchers because it focuses on integrating these ideas into our daily lives. For so many people, managing money is a taboo subject, a source of shame or embarrassment. People tend not to talk about it with others. And that's a recipe for disaster."

Jason is very big on statistics and Visa does lots of surveys. "Many people are fundamentally uninformed," Jason told me. Visa did a survey about credit scores, the number that measures your credit worthiness based on your bill payment history. The results were astonishing. Forty-seven percent of the respondents believed that their age impacts their credit score (it doesn't!); 32 percent believe it is impacted by where you live (it isn't!); 27 percent thought the ability to speak English affects their score (no!), and 24 percent thought both race and gender impacts your score (no!). (Later in this chapter, I'll explain what your credit score is, how it is measured, and how you can make it better.)

"If you don't know what factors affect your credit score, you can't take steps to improve it," Jason said. "If you think gender is a factor, you will assume you can't change it and won't devote any energy to changing it. But that three-digit number has an enormous impact on getting loans, getting jobs, getting housing . . . it's a huge, real-world, real-life tangible thing."

Wow, he is right about that. What is more amazing is how even a small amount of education can impact behavior. For example, Visa recently worked with Wells Fargo bank on an education initiative for college students who were first-time credit cardholders. The idea was to improve student cardholders' understanding of responsible borrowing and credit management and to measure the effects of this education on their credit card behavior. Visa created the program for Wells Fargo and named it Practical Money Skills for Life.

Wells Fargo sent out an invitation to 78,000 new credit cardholders to come to a website to take two lessons and quizzes designed to increase the awareness of the importance of building strong credit. To gauge the value of the program, they set up a control group of 3,000 randomly selected students who had also just gotten credit cards but had received nothing more than standard cardholder treatment.

Nearly 7 percent or 5,500 students responded to the offer, which is a good response for a direct mail campaign. And the results of even this small bit of learning were dramatic. Those who completed the course had *42.6 percent fewer instances of late fees and over-limit charges and this same group had 27 percent lower revolving balances than the control group.* And the results were not based on lower usage of credit cards. In fact, the people who completed the course spent 33 percent *more* on their cards than the control group.

This is a validation of what I've believed all along: a smart, informed consumer is less likely to get into financial trouble.

Kim Appleberg, senior director of human resources for McDonald's, has launched a nationwide initiative incorporating Wealth Watchers to address the financial education needs of its employees. The program, Kim says, is an enhancement to McDonald's benefit packages and it addresses what she sees as a crucial need for employees who are mostly young and starting out in their lives.

"We had been hearing from various feedback channels that the topic of financial education was of increasing interest to our employees," Kim said. "The average age of our employees is twenty-seven. Many are just starting out, buying their first home or renting their first apartments, starting a family, and this is an opportunity to help them in an area they haven't had access to before.

"In many ways, it is similar to health care education. We provide access to programs for that as well. In terms of financial education, we offer employees access to 401K plans, employee stock purchase plans, things like that. And until they understand the basics of finance, they don't understand that they can participate and the value of participating in these benefits. We see a need for a basic foundation: budgeting, why it's important to save, how do I start saving . . . things like that.

"If employees are able to manage their finances in a successful way, that often will translate into more presence at work, less worry about paying bills, about the utilities being shut off. So we see greater productivity, greater stability, a greater retention rate at work. It benefits the employees and it benefits the company."

Are you listening, Corporate America? There is opportunity here. A financially savvy employee is a better, more productive, more focused employee. Jason Alderman has seen evidence of this. In the midst of a terrible economic downturn that has done so much damage to so many people, there has been one silver lining: "People are really paying attention to financial education more than ever," Jason said. "After an earthquake, people rush to make sure they are insured. In the same way, people are getting more focused on getting their financial house in order so they can prevent the next crisis."

I've seen and heard all kinds of ideas, good and bad, for how to fix a system that is clearly broken. I've met good bankers and bad bankers, people who get it, and people who live in a rose-colored bubble.

The road to the kwan is littered with the debris of ignorance and miscommunication. Wealth Watchers is an easy and effective way to take control of your finances and attain some peace of both mind and wallet. But the vast American complacency about financial literacy has to change if we are going to make significant progress in this vital part of our lives. We need to see financial literacy become a mandate in schools and in the workplace. Companies like McDonald's and Visa serve as excellent examples of what I call "enlightened self-interest" in which doing good results in doing well. A company with financially literate employees is likely to have happier, more productive employees not consumed by scraping together the next mortgage payment or putting food on the table.

Every bank, and especially banks that received federal bailout money, should provide financial literacy programs for their employees and their customers. If we are counting on the lenders to fix themselves, reaching out a comforting hand to unsophisticated borrowers, we may wait a long time.

Writing in *The New Yorker* of April 13, 2009, in an article entitled "I.O.U.," Jill Lepore provided a sobering history of debt and the advent of bankruptcy laws in our country. I think her assessment is worth considering. Americans embraced bankruptcy laws because it made taking risks less risky. In business and in life, we are risk takers and that has helped build the world's biggest and most successful economy. But everything comes with a price.

"Consumer debt, which stands at two and half trillion dollars, has been the engine of the American economy since the 1970s and, arguably, longer. Buying on credit has been, for at least the past half century, pitched to the American people as a civic responsibility. We keep buying and spending and overextending and forgiving debts; we keep forgetting how we came to accumulate them; we can't seem to remember that bad times follow good; we lack the fortitude supplied by a bracing history. There are a thousand bankruptcy lawyers working in Manhattan today. There will be more tomorrow; they peddle pastlessness. But sometimes there's profit in looking back, and reckoning our accounts."

Maybe this current economic crisis will help spur some national introspection about finances. My guess is that the next up cycle will indeed make many people forget the pain they're feeling now. At least we can take this opportunity to look at ourselves in a very clear mirror and take control of our own financial lives. Everyone who's tried using the Wealth Watchers journal has commented on how much less money they waste. Tracking your expenses is an effort, but it's an effort that will be worthwhile for anyone who thinks they could manage their money more carefully. And really, isn't that all of us?

TAKING PERSONAL RESPONSIBILITY: A CHECKLIST

As you get ready to start your journal, it's comforting to know that you couldn't have picked a better time to embrace a new outlook and attitude toward tracking your money. Change is always hard but the alternative—doing nothing—is not an option in this financial environment. So the best course, and it usually is, is to take control for yourself. Below is a checklist I put together entitled "A Call to Action for Consumers" that you should complete before you start your Wealth Watchers journal in the next chapter. These are the steps you need to take on the road to financial health:

1. **Get organized.** Keep all receipts and bills in one place where you can easily locate them.
2. **Make sure your partner is on board.** Money problems are the number one cause of divorce. This will be simpler if your partner embraces the idea that every day and every dollar really do make a difference in reaching your financial goals.
3. **Develop a coding system for expenses to share with your family.**
4. **Define and understand the difference between fixed, semi-fixed, and discretionary expenses.**
5. **Rigorously challenge your fixed and semi-fixed expenses.** Reduce both wherever possible.
6. **Make your budget.**
7. **Know your DDI.** Use the worksheet on page 142 in the Journal to understand how much money you can spend every day without going into debt.
8. **Find out your credit score and if it is under 700, make it higher.** *Don't skip this step!* As Jason Alderman pointed out earlier, a credit score is a vital financial measurement in people's lives and it's just astonishing how few people even know they have a credit score, let alone what impact it has. Surveys show that as many as 70 percent of Americans don't know they have a credit score. But mortgage lenders and

Here's how a credit score breaks down, according to CBS's *The Early Show* financial adviser Ray Martin:

- **35 percent: payment history**—if you have a long and clean history of making payments on time, for a mortgage, a car loan, credit cards, your score will reflect this. It is one of the first things lenders look for.
- **30 percent: amount owed**—how much you owe at any given time relative to your available credit. If you have maxed out your credit cards and other loans, you are considered a higher risk for late payments.
- **15 percent: length of credit history**—how long you've had viable credit products is one way lenders determine your reliability.
- **10 percent: new credit**—if you open many new credit products in a short period of time, it can lower your credit score and lenders will be concerned.
- **10 percent: types of credit in use**—lenders look at the mix of credit you have, from credit cards to mortgages, and this can impact your credit score.

You can also avoid accumulating a bunch of new credit cards in a short time. Some experts suggest having no more than five credit cards at one time using less than 50 percent of your available credit limit on each card. If you do have a late payment, you should contact the lender and ask to have the late payment removed from your record. Sometimes they will, sometimes they won't. It's worth pursuing to avoid the hit on your credit score.

According to Visa's Jason Alderman, you should review your credit reports. You can order one free report each year from each of the three major credit bureaus at www.annualcreditreport.com. He recommends that you check for fraud or errors that could lower your score. You can also estimate your score using a free FICO score estimator at What's My Score, a financial literacy program run by Visa (www.whatsmyscore.org/estimator).

most financial institutions use this three-digit number to determine whether they'll give you a loan. It's also used by employers, landlords, and utility companies to evaluate your reliability and financial integrity.

Your credit score is called a FICO score (it was named after Fair Isaac Corporation, the company that created the number) and it is a number between 300 and 850. The higher your number, the better—the less of a credit risk for lenders. A higher FICO number means you are more likely to make your loan payments and make them on time. Most lenders believe that a score of 720 or higher is as good as it needs to be. There is an abundance of information on credit scores online and it is worth the minimal cost to get your score so you know where you stand and what you must do to improve it. As Jason's survey pointed out, your gender, age, race, income, and location have nothing to do with your score. I can assure you of one thing: if you follow the Wealth Watchers program religiously, you should be able to raise your credit score significantly.

The obvious question for people with low scores is: Can I make them better? The answer is: Absolutely, and in some obvious ways. Paying your bills on time for a long period of time is the best way to raise your score. Avoid late payments that can damage your score and result in greatly increased interest rates. If you have large credit card balances, you can raise your credit score by paying down the balance. Try to use the smallest percentage of your available credit as possible.

9. **Set up a bill payment system that works for you and your partner.** This will prevent late payments. There's no one system that will work for everyone. Some people pay bills online while others phone in their payments and yet others send checks. I keep a list of every bill we have each month and what date each payment is due. I have almost all of our payments automatically deducted from our checking account so I really just have to make sure that there's enough money in the account as each bill comes due.

Some people actually write a check for their bills as soon as they receive the bill. Even though that payment may not be due for another two or three weeks they just go ahead and put it in the mail so they don't have to think about it. That's not possible if you're living paycheck to paycheck, but paying as you go is something worth striving for. Online billpay is certainly a great way to make sure your bills are paid on time. Tech savvy people are also very likely to check their bank statements online fairly often which fits right in with the Wealth Watchers theory that it's important to know your numbers . . . including your bank balance.

10. **Know your small leaks.** Everyone has a weakness when it comes to spending money. By identifying yours—you always buy a second pair of shoes when you only need the

first, you always order that second bottle of wine at a restaurant, you book a winter vacation for the family even if the money isn't available—you will make significant changes to your spending habits.

11. **Set up a simple old-fashioned savings account.** It's bad luck to think that nothing will ever go wrong in your life. Maintaining a savings account is a great way to be prepared for a financial setback. Ask your banker to automatically transfer a certain amount (10% is a good number) each month from your checking account to your savings account. It's the best way to make saving money effortless.

12. **Have your paycheck deposited directly.** If a check doesn't pass through your hands you'll be less likely to waste the money. Even better, you won't be hit with a check processing fee.

13. **Commit to saving an additional percentage of your income for retirement.** Even if it's a small increase, every little bit will make a difference. Make sure it is automatically deposited in a retirement account or 401K. If you are self-employed, you should open a SEP IRA, the equivalent of a 401K. Talk to a certified financial planner about the best plan for you.

14. **Recognize the power of compound interest and teach your children about it as well.** If you look at any chart that calculates compound interest, you will be astounded how much you will have saved by your retirement age if you start young. Even if you're not so young anymore, it's better to start late than not at all.

Actually, every working adult should follow these two formulas: "Better late than never," and "Better something than nothing." Maybe 10 percent is too much for you to save right now. Even if you start by saving $25 from each paycheck, something is better than nothing. The same is true for a retirement account. There's nothing wrong with starting out with a small contribution from each paycheck. Just try to contribute more to your retirement account every chance you get, especially if there is any kind of matching contribution from your employer. That is free money!

15. **Share your goal.** People are much more likely to succeed if they share their goal with another person. Share your financial goals with a trusted friend or family member. You can even start your own "money club" to share ideas and resources for being better with money. Group encouragement is known to help people reach their goals. At Weight Watchers meetings I always felt like I learned so much from the other people attending the meetings. I loved it when people would talk about what strategies worked for them.

   A money group will give you new ideas for saving money as well as moral support. You'll be surprised at what tips people are willing to share.

16. **Keep your journal with your spending money.** Your journal and your spending need to be joined at the hip. The journal is the new lens with which to view your financial life. Use it to simplify and stabilize your financial life, because it is only from this sturdy base that you can welcome the kwan into your life.

PART II
A JOURNAL

In sports, there's a saying that it's hard to tell the players without a scorecard.

With money, there's a reality that it's tough to have a scorecard when there are so many players:

- Credit Cards
- Debit Cards
- Checks
- Cash withdrawals

Even worse, imagine two people using all of the above without sharing information on a regular basis. Wealth Watchers will help you keep an accurate scorecard.

Wealth Watchers allows participants to:
- share useful tips.
- offer encouragement for spending less money than you make.
- track where the money goes that you do spend.

GETTING ORGANIZED

Set aside one place where all of your bills, bank statements, and any other financial information will be stored: a file cabinet, drawer, folder, or whatever works for you.

UNDERSTANDING YOUR INCOME AND EXPENSES

How much money do you really have to spend? You can look over your past bank statements and credit card statements to get a feel for where your money has been going vs. where your money has to go. The Monthly Budget will help you pull together these numbers.

COMPLETING THE MONTHLY BUDGET

Monthly Net Income—List all available income you receive each month.

Monthly Fixed Expenses—List every expense that you have that is the same each month.

Monthly Semi-Fixed Expenses—List every expense that you have each month that varies in amount, such as utilities.
When listing both your Fixed and Semi-Fixed Expenses, ask yourself if any of the payments can be lowered.

REVIEWING YOUR FINANCIAL PICTURE
Keep in mind necessary expenses such as food, shelter, clothing, transportation, medical needs, education or child care must have priority in your planning. Subtract your Total Fixed and Semi-Fixed Expenses from your Total Net Income to reach your Monthly Disposable Income (MDI), otherwise known as spending money.

DETERMINING YOUR DISPOSABLE INCOME
Disposable Income is income available each month after paying your Fixed and Semi-Fixed Expenses. The Monthly Budget will provide the amount of your Disposable Income as projected for the year. That number will be divided by 365 to give you a daily target that will be known as your Daily Disposable Income, or DDI. Keep in mind "The Power of 365." Any savings times 365 is a worthwhile goal.

Sample Monthly Budget/DDI Determination

Monthly Net Income

Income 1	$	2,400
Income 2	$	2,400
Other Income	$	0
Total Net Income	$	**4,800**

Monthly Fixed Expenses

Savings	$	300
Mortgage / Rent	$	1,156
Car Payment	$	150
Car/Home Insurance	$	169
Life Insurance	$	131
Day Care	$	350

Monthly Semi-Fixed Expenses

Cable / Phone	$	100*
Electric Bill	$	150*
Heating Bill	$	150*
Total Fixed & Semi-Fixed Expenses	$	**2,656**

Monthly Disposable Income (MDI) .... $ 2,144

(Total Net Income minus Total Fixed & Semi-Fixed Expenses)

Yearly Disposable Income .... $ 25,728

(Monthly Disposable Income multiplied by 12)

Daily Disposable Income (DDI) .... $ | 70 |

(Yearly Disposable Income ÷ 365)

Remember: "Every day and every dollar make a difference" ®

* Average (Actual figure varies from month to month)

Monthly Budget/DDI Determination *

Monthly Net Income

Income 1.. $_____

Income 2.. $_____

Other Income .... $_____

Total Net Income.. $_____

Monthly Fixed Expenses

.... $_____

.... $_____

.... $_____

.... $_____

.... $_____

.... $_____

.... $_____

Monthly Semi-Fixed Expenses

.... $_____ **

.... $_____ **

.... $_____ **

.... $_____ **

Total Fixed & Semi-Fixed Expenses .... $_____

Monthly Disposable Income (MDI).................................... $_____

(Total Net Income minus Total Fixed & Semi-Fixed Expenses)

Yearly Disposable Income .... $_____

(Monthly Disposable Income multiplied by 12)

Daily Disposable Income (DDI).................................... $ [   ]

(Yearly Disposable Income ÷ 365)

* Help with determining your DDI is available through www.ewealthwatchers.com
** Average (Actual figure varies from month to month)

WHAT IS YOUR GOAL?

- Saving for vacation, education, home ownership or retirement?
- Spending less money than you make?
- Knowing where your money goes?
- _____

Every day and every dollar can help you meet your goals.

JOURNALING

We all need a reality check. Recording your daily spending will help you understand where your money goes. It forces a "think before you spend" moment. The only items that should be journaled are those expenditures other than Fixed and Semi-Fixed Expenses. These items would include groceries, transportation, clothing, restaurants, medical expenses, etc. Expenses such as travel, gifts, luxury items, etc. should be the target for better planning. *You can have almost anything you want as long as you plan ahead and save for it.*

Use of Codes—The following codes may be helpful when journaling your expenses.

List the method of payment first and then list what was purchased. Feel free to create whatever code system works best for you.

C	Cash	**G**	Groceries
CC	Credit Card	**R**	Restaurant
DC	Debit Card	**MD**	Medical Expense
CK	Check	**T**	Transportation

Daily Total—Add your daily expenditures and record the total amount for each day. Do not include expenditures that are part of your Fixed and Semi-Fixed Expense List. They have already been factored into the determination of your Disposable Income.

DDI GOAL IS $ ____70____

Monday

Code/Description/Expense

cc / groceries (G) / 112

c / restaurant (R) / 3

c / gas (T) / 21

DAILY TOTAL   _136_

Tuesday

Code/Description/Expense

cc / gift (GI) / 22

c / fast food (FF) / 14

dc / miscellaneous (M) / 21

DAILY TOTAL   _57_

Wednesday

Code/Description/Expense

c / fast food (FF) / 10

cc / restaurant (R) / 44

DAILY TOTAL   _54_

Thursday

Code/Description/Expense

c / allowance (A) / 40

c / restaurant (R) / 10

DAILY TOTAL   _50_

—SAMPLE—

Friday

Code/Description/Expense

cc / restaurant (R) / 22

c / drink (D) / 4

DAILY TOTAL _26_

Saturday

Code/Description/Expense

c / sitter / 20

cc / fast food (FF) / 13

DAILY TOTAL _33_

Sunday

Code/Description/Expense

cc / gift (GI) / 11

c / restaurant (R) / 43

DAILY TOTAL _54_

WEEKLY SUMMARY

Weekly Total of Expenses (Add Daily Totals)

My Expenses ___410___ + Partner Expenses ___0___

Total ___410___

Actual Average Daily Total of Expenses
(Weekly Total of Expenses ÷ 7) ___59___

Under (+)/Over (-) Budget per day
(DDI Goal minus Actual Average
Daily Total of Expenses) ___+11___

Weekly Total—Add your daily totals for the week and record that figure in the Weekly Summary box at the bottom of that week's journal. Include your partner's figures if applicable. Your average daily total will be the weekly total divided by seven.

Monthly Total—Add your daily totals for the month and record the figure on the respective Monthly Budget Summary located at the back of this journal. The average daily total will be the monthly total divided by the number of days in that month.

Quarterly Total—Add your monthly totals for the quarter and record that figure on the respective Quarterly Budget Summary located at the back of this journal. The average daily total will be the quarterly total divided by the number of days in that quarter.

How Well Did You Do?—The difference between your DDI goal and your actual average daily total of expenses will show you if you are staying on track. Were you over or under your targeted Daily Disposable Income (DDI)? A plus (+) sign next to your number would indicate that you had a savings of that much per day. A minus (-) sign next to your number would indicate that you overspent by that much per day. *Any savings times 365 will be a worthwhile goal.*

FREQUENTLY ASKED QUESTIONS

What if my spouse/partner and I are each using a different journal? Sunday is the day of reconciliation. Compare both journals and add both sets of expenses to reach a weekly total.

How do I record a returned purchase? Any return should be credited to the day it was returned. Put a plus sign in front of any amount to remind you that it is a credit, not an expense.

How do I record using a gift card? You don't need to journal the use of a gift card.

How do I record using a gift of cash? You don't need to record spending cash that was a gift. If the cash is placed into savings, you should record it as a credit on the date it was received.

How do I record an expense that will be reimbursed? Any reimbursable expense should be circled to remind you to collect for that expense. Once reimbursed put a plus sign in front of that amount to remind you that it is a credit, not an expense.

Remember:"Every day and every dollar make a difference" ®

TIPS FOR BEING A GOOD WEALTH WATCHER®

1. Spend less money than you make.

2. Always look for a better alternative.
- Don't use an ATM outside of your bank's system.
- Pack your lunch occasionally instead of eating out too often.
- When possible, use public transportation or share travel expenses.
- Plan meals in advance.
- Pick up carry-out instead of paying for delivery.
- Borrow books and movies from the library.
- Shop with a list instead of impulse shopping.
- Go for a walk instead of going shopping.

3. Set up direct deposit for your paycheck.
You'll be less likely to waste your paycheck if it goes directly into your bank account. You'll also avoid the high fees associated with payday loans.

4. Open a savings account.
Meet with a banker about automatically transferring a set amount each month from your checking account to a savings account. Any amount is better than nothing. If you need a target, you should put 5 to 10% of your income into a non-retirement savings account. Your savings account should pay for emergencies, travel, new cars, education, etc. Some people set up separate accounts for different goals. Find a system that works for you and have your banker automatically transfer the appropriate amounts to the different accounts each month.

5. Ask your banker how you can avoid any overdraft fees.

Many banks offer services that protect you should you overdraw your account.

6. Open a retirement account.

Most employers offer direct deposits from your paycheck to a retirement account. Take advantage of any retirement plans to the greatest extent possible.

7. Shop locally.

The sales tax will help support services in your community.

8. Be Safe.

- Don't cut corners when it comes to your personal safety.

9. Understand the difference between good debt and bad debt.

- A mortgage for an **affordable** home is good debt.
- Buying "things" on credit and carrying a balance is bad debt.
- If you buy a home, try to pay it off as soon as possible and try to preserve the equity in your home.

10. Live Smart™.

- You can have almost anything you want as long as you plan and save for it.
- Balance your savings goals with living a balanced life.
- Be a good example for your family.
- Learn from others who are better with money.
- Share ideas for being smarter with money.

NOTES

_____

_____

_____

_____

_____

_____

_____

_____

_____

_____

_____

_____

_____

_____

NOTES

_____

_____

_____

_____

_____

_____

_____

_____

_____

_____

_____

_____

_____

_____

DDI GOAL IS $ _____

Monday	/	/	
Code/Description/Expense			
DAILY TOTAL			

Tuesday	/	/	
Code/Description/Expense			
DAILY TOTAL			

Wednesday	/	/	
Code/Description/Expense			
DAILY TOTAL			

Thursday	/	/	
Code/Description/Expense			
DAILY TOTAL			

Friday   /   /

Code/Description/Expense

DAILY TOTAL

Saturday   /   /

Code/Description/Expense

DAILY TOTAL

Sunday   /   /

Code/Description/Expense

DAILY TOTAL

WEEKLY SUMMARY — Week of _____ / _____ / _____

Weekly Total of Expenses (Add Daily Totals)

           My Expenses _____ + Partner Expenses _____

                                        Total _____

           Actual Average Daily Total of Expenses

           (Weekly Total of Expenses ÷ 7)   _____

           Under (+)/Over (-) Budget per day

           (DDI Goal minus Actual Average

           Daily Total of Expenses)   _____

DDI GOAL IS $ _____

Monday	/	/	
Code/Description/Expense			
DAILY TOTAL			

Tuesday	/	/	
Code/Description/Expense			
DAILY TOTAL			

Wednesday	/	/	
Code/Description/Expense			
DAILY TOTAL			

Thursday	/	/	
Code/Description/Expense			
DAILY TOTAL			

Friday / /

Code/Description/Expense

DAILY TOTAL

Saturday / /

Code/Description/Expense

DAILY TOTAL

Sunday / /

Code/Description/Expense

DAILY TOTAL

WEEKLY SUMMARY — Week of _____ / _____ / _____

Weekly Total of Expenses (Add Daily Totals)

My Expenses _____ + Partner Expenses _____

Total _____

Actual Average Daily Total of Expenses
(Weekly Total of Expenses + 7) _____

Under (+)/Over (-) Budget per day
(DDI Goal minus Actual Average
Daily Total of Expenses) _____

DDI GOAL IS $ _____

| **Monday** | / | / |

Code/Description/Expense

DAILY TOTAL

| **Tuesday** | / | / |

Code/Description/Expense

DAILY TOTAL

| **Wednesday** | / | / |

Code/Description/Expense

DAILY TOTAL

| **Thursday** | / | / |

Code/Description/Expense

DAILY TOTAL

Friday / /

Code/Description/Expense

DAILY TOTAL

Saturday / /

Code/Description/Expense

DAILY TOTAL

Sunday / /

Code/Description/Expense

DAILY TOTAL

WEEKLY SUMMARY — Week of _____ / _____ / _____

Weekly Total of Expenses (Add Daily Totals)

My Expenses _____ + Partner Expenses _____

Total _____

Actual Average Daily Total of Expenses
(Weekly Total of Expenses ÷ 7) _____

Under (+)/Over (-) Budget per day
(DDI Goal minus Actual Average
Daily Total of Expenses) _____

DDI GOAL IS $ _____

Monday   /   /

Code/Description/Expense

DAILY TOTAL

Tuesday   /   /

Code/Description/Expense

DAILY TOTAL

Wednesday   /   /

Code/Description/Expense

DAILY TOTAL

Thursday   /   /

Code/Description/Expense

DAILY TOTAL

Friday   /   /

Code/Description/Expense

DAILY TOTAL

Saturday   /   /

Code/Description/Expense

DAILY TOTAL

Sunday   /   /

Code/Description/Expense

DAILY TOTAL

WEEKLY SUMMARY — Week of _____ / _____ / _____

Weekly Total of Expenses (Add Daily Totals)

My Expenses _____ + Partner Expenses _____

Total _____

Actual Average Daily Total of Expenses
(Weekly Total of Expenses ÷ 7) _____

Under (+)/Over (-) Budget per day
(DDI Goal minus Actual Average
Daily Total of Expenses) _____

DDI GOAL IS $ _____

Monday / /

Code/Description/Expense

DAILY TOTAL

Tuesday / /

Code/Description/Expense

DAILY TOTAL

Wednesday / /

Code/Description/Expense

DAILY TOTAL

Thursday / /

Code/Description/Expense

DAILY TOTAL

160

Friday / /

Code/Description/Expense

DAILY TOTAL

Saturday / /

Code/Description/Expense

DAILY TOTAL

Sunday / /

Code/Description/Expense

DAILY TOTAL

WEEKLY SUMMARY — Week of _____ / _____ / _____

Weekly Total of Expenses (Add Daily Totals)

My Expenses _____ + Partner Expenses _____

Total _____

Actual Average Daily Total of Expenses
(Weekly Total of Expenses ÷ 7) _____

Under (+)/Over (-) Budget per day
(DDI Goal minus Actual Average
Daily Total of Expenses) _____

DDI GOAL IS $ _____

Monday	/	/	

Code/Description/Expense

DAILY TOTAL

Tuesday	/	/	

Code/Description/Expense

DAILY TOTAL

Wednesday	/	/	

Code/Description/Expense

DAILY TOTAL

Thursday	/	/	

Code/Description/Expense

DAILY TOTAL

Friday   /   /

Code/Description/Expense

DAILY TOTAL

Saturday   /   /

Code/Description/Expense

DAILY TOTAL

Sunday   /   /

Code/Description/Expense

DAILY TOTAL

WEEKLY SUMMARY — Week of _____ / _____ / _____

Weekly Total of Expenses (Add Daily Totals)

    My Expenses _____ + Partner Expenses _____

                                         Total _____

        Actual Average Daily Total of Expenses

        (Weekly Total of Expenses ÷ 7)   _____

        Under (+)/Over (-) Budget per day

        (DDI Goal minus Actual Average

        Daily Total of Expenses)   _____

DDI GOAL IS $ _____

| Monday | / | / |

Code/Description/Expense

DAILY TOTAL

| Tuesday | / | / |

Code/Description/Expense

DAILY TOTAL

| Wednesday | / | / |

Code/Description/Expense

DAILY TOTAL

| Thursday | / | / |

Code/Description/Expense

DAILY TOTAL

Friday ___ / ___ / ___

Code/Description/Expense

DAILY TOTAL

Saturday ___ / ___ / ___

Code/Description/Expense

DAILY TOTAL

Sunday ___ / ___ / ___

Code/Description/Expense

DAILY TOTAL

WEEKLY SUMMARY — Week of ___ / ___ / ___

Weekly Total of Expenses (Add Daily Totals)

My Expenses _____ + Partner Expenses _____

Total _____

Actual Average Daily Total of Expenses
(Weekly Total of Expenses ÷ 7) _____

Under (+)/Over (-) Budget per day
(DDI Goal minus Actual Average
Daily Total of Expenses) _____

DDI GOAL IS $ _____

Monday   /   /

Code/Description/Expense

_____

_____

_____

_____

DAILY TOTAL

Tuesday   /   /

Code/Description/Expense

_____

_____

_____

_____

DAILY TOTAL

Wednesday   /   /

Code/Description/Expense

_____

_____

_____

_____

DAILY TOTAL

Thursday   /   /

Code/Description/Expense

_____

_____

_____

_____

DAILY TOTAL

Friday   /   /

Code/Description/Expense

DAILY TOTAL

Saturday   /   /

Code/Description/Expense

DAILY TOTAL

Sunday   /   /

Code/Description/Expense

DAILY TOTAL

WEEKLY SUMMARY — Week of _____ / _____ / _____

Weekly Total of Expenses (Add Daily Totals)

My Expenses _____ + Partner Expenses _____

Total _____

Actual Average Daily Total of Expenses
(Weekly Total of Expenses ÷ 7) _____

Under (+)/Over (-) Budget per day
(DDI Goal minus Actual Average
Daily Total of Expenses) _____

DDI GOAL IS $ _____

Monday	/	/

Code/Description/Expense

DAILY TOTAL

Tuesday	/	/

Code/Description/Expense

DAILY TOTAL

Wednesday	/	/

Code/Description/Expense

DAILY TOTAL

Thursday	/	/

Code/Description/Expense

DAILY TOTAL

Friday	/	/	

Code/Description/Expense

DAILY TOTAL

Saturday	/	/	

Code/Description/Expense

DAILY TOTAL

Sunday	/	/	

Code/Description/Expense

DAILY TOTAL

WEEKLY SUMMARY — Week of _____ / _____ / _____

Weekly Total of Expenses (Add Daily Totals)
My Expenses _____ + Partner Expenses _____
Total _____

Actual Average Daily Total of Expenses
(Weekly Total of Expenses ÷ 7) _____

Under (+)/Over (-) Budget per day
(DDI Goal minus Actual Average
Daily Total of Expenses) _____

DDI GOAL IS $ _____

Monday	/	/

Code/Description/Expense

DAILY TOTAL

Tuesday	/	/

Code/Description/Expense

DAILY TOTAL

Wednesday	/	/

Code/Description/Expense

DAILY TOTAL

Thursday	/	/

Code/Description/Expense

DAILY TOTAL

Friday / /

Code/Description/Expense

DAILY TOTAL

Saturday / /

Code/Description/Expense

DAILY TOTAL

Sunday / /

Code/Description/Expense

DAILY TOTAL

WEEKLY SUMMARY — Week of _____ / _____ / _____

Weekly Total of Expenses (Add Daily Totals)
        My Expenses _____ + Partner Expenses _____
                                                Total _____

        Actual Average Daily Total of Expenses
        (Weekly Total of Expenses ÷ 7)   _____

        Under (+)/Over (-) Budget per day
        (DDI Goal minus Actual Average
        Daily Total of Expenses)   _____

DDI GOAL IS $ _____

Monday	/	/	

Code/Description/Expense

DAILY TOTAL

Tuesday	/	/	

Code/Description/Expense

DAILY TOTAL

Wednesday	/	/	

Code/Description/Expense

DAILY TOTAL

Thursday	/	/	

Code/Description/Expense

DAILY TOTAL

Friday ___ / ___ / ___

Code/Description/Expense

DAILY TOTAL

Saturday ___ / ___ / ___

Code/Description/Expense

DAILY TOTAL

Sunday ___ / ___ / ___

Code/Description/Expense

DAILY TOTAL

WEEKLY SUMMARY — Week of ___ / ___ / ___

Weekly Total of Expenses (Add Daily Totals)

My Expenses _____ + Partner Expenses _____

Total _____

Actual Average Daily Total of Expenses
(Weekly Total of Expenses ÷ 7)   _____

Under (+)/Over (-) Budget per day
(DDI Goal minus Actual Average
Daily Total of Expenses)   _____

DDI GOAL IS $ _____

Monday	/	/

Code/Description/Expense

DAILY TOTAL

Tuesday	/	/

Code/Description/Expense

DAILY TOTAL

Wednesday	/	/

Code/Description/Expense

DAILY TOTAL

Thursday	/	/

Code/Description/Expense

DAILY TOTAL

Friday / /

Code/Description/Expense

DAILY TOTAL

Saturday / /

Code/Description/Expense

DAILY TOTAL

Sunday / /

Code/Description/Expense

DAILY TOTAL

WEEKLY SUMMARY — Week of ____ / ____ / ____

Weekly Total of Expenses (Add Daily Totals)

My Expenses _____ + Partner Expenses _____

Total _____

Actual Average Daily Total of Expenses
(Weekly Total of Expenses ÷ 7) _____

Under (+)/Over (-) Budget per day
(DDI Goal minus Actual Average
Daily Total of Expenses) _____

DDI GOAL IS
$ _____

Monday   /   /

Code/Description/Expense

DAILY TOTAL

Tuesday   /   /

Code/Description/Expense

DAILY TOTAL

Wednesday   /   /

Code/Description/Expense

DAILY TOTAL

Thursday   /   /

Code/Description/Expense

DAILY TOTAL

Friday / /

Code/Description/Expense

DAILY TOTAL

Saturday / /

Code/Description/Expense

DAILY TOTAL

Sunday / /

Code/Description/Expense

DAILY TOTAL

WEEKLY SUMMARY — Week of _____ / _____ / _____

Weekly Total of Expenses (Add Daily Totals)

My Expenses _____ + Partner Expenses _____

Total _____

Actual Average Daily Total of Expenses
(Weekly Total of Expenses ÷ 7) _____

Under (+)/Over (-) Budget per day
(DDI Goal minus Actual Average
Daily Total of Expenses) _____

DDI GOAL IS $ _____

Monday   /   /

Code/Description/Expense

DAILY TOTAL

Tuesday   /   /

Code/Description/Expense

DAILY TOTAL

Wednesday   /   /

Code/Description/Expense

DAILY TOTAL

Thursday   /   /

Code/Description/Expense

DAILY TOTAL

Friday / /

Code/Description/Expense

DAILY TOTAL

Saturday / /

Code/Description/Expense

DAILY TOTAL

Sunday / /

Code/Description/Expense

DAILY TOTAL

WEEKLY SUMMARY — Week of ＿＿ / ＿＿ / ＿＿

Weekly Total of Expenses (Add Daily Totals)

My Expenses ＿＿＿＿＿＿ + Partner Expenses ＿＿＿＿＿

Total ＿＿＿＿

Actual Average Daily Total of Expenses
(Weekly Total of Expenses ÷ 7) ＿＿＿＿

Under (+)/Over (-) Budget per day
(DDI Goal minus Actual Average
Daily Total of Expenses) ＿＿＿＿

DDI GOAL IS $ _____

Monday / /

Code/Description/Expense

DAILY TOTAL

Tuesday / /

Code/Description/Expense

DAILY TOTAL

Wednesday / /

Code/Description/Expense

DAILY TOTAL

Thursday / /

Code/Description/Expense

DAILY TOTAL

Friday / /

Code/Description/Expense

DAILY TOTAL

Saturday / /

Code/Description/Expense

DAILY TOTAL

Sunday / /

Code/Description/Expense

DAILY TOTAL

WEEKLY SUMMARY — Week of _____ / _____ / _____

Weekly Total of Expenses (Add Daily Totals)

      My Expenses _____ + Partner Expenses _____

                                         Total _____

      Actual Average Daily Total of Expenses

      (Weekly Total of Expenses ÷ 7)   _____

      Under (+)/Over (-) Budget per day

      (DDI Goal minus Actual Average

      Daily Total of Expenses)   _____

DDI GOAL IS $ _____

Monday	/	/		

Code/Description/Expense

DAILY TOTAL

Tuesday	/	/		

Code/Description/Expense

DAILY TOTAL

Wednesday	/	/		

Code/Description/Expense

DAILY TOTAL

Thursday	/	/		

Code/Description/Expense

DAILY TOTAL

Friday / /

Code/Description/Expense

DAILY TOTAL

Saturday / /

Code/Description/Expense

DAILY TOTAL

Sunday / /

Code/Description/Expense

DAILY TOTAL

WEEKLY SUMMARY — Week of _____ / _____ / _____

Weekly Total of Expenses (Add Daily Totals)

My Expenses _____ + Partner Expenses _____

Total _____

Actual Average Daily Total of Expenses
(Weekly Total of Expenses ÷ 7) _____

Under (+)/Over (-) Budget per day
(DDI Goal minus Actual Average
Daily Total of Expenses) _____

DDI GOAL IS $ _____

Monday	/	/	
Code/Description/Expense			
DAILY TOTAL			

Tuesday	/	/	
Code/Description/Expense			
DAILY TOTAL			

Wednesday	/	/	
Code/Description/Expense			
DAILY TOTAL			

Thursday	/	/	
Code/Description/Expense			
DAILY TOTAL			

Friday ___ / ___ / ___

Code/Description/Expense

DAILY TOTAL

Saturday ___ / ___ / ___

Code/Description/Expense

DAILY TOTAL

Sunday ___ / ___ / ___

Code/Description/Expense

DAILY TOTAL

WEEKLY SUMMARY — Week of ___ / ___ / ___

Weekly Total of Expenses (Add Daily Totals)

My Expenses _____ + Partner Expenses _____

Total _____

Actual Average Daily Total of Expenses
(Weekly Total of Expenses ÷ 7) _____

Under (+)/Over (-) Budget per day
(DDI Goal minus Actual Average
Daily Total of Expenses) _____

DDI GOAL IS $ _____

Monday	/	/	
Code/Description/Expense			

DAILY TOTAL

Tuesday	/	/	
Code/Description/Expense			

DAILY TOTAL

Wednesday	/	/	
Code/Description/Expense			

DAILY TOTAL

Thursday	/	/	
Code/Description/Expense			

DAILY TOTAL

Friday / /

Code/Description/Expense

DAILY TOTAL

Saturday / /

Code/Description/Expense

DAILY TOTAL

Sunday / /

Code/Description/Expense

DAILY TOTAL

WEEKLY SUMMARY — Week of _____ / _____ / _____

Weekly Total of Expenses (Add Daily Totals)

My Expenses _____ + Partner Expenses _____

Total _____

Actual Average Daily Total of Expenses
(Weekly Total of Expenses ÷ 7) _____

Under (+)/Over (-) Budget per day
(DDI Goal minus Actual Average
Daily Total of Expenses) _____

DDI GOAL IS $ _____

Monday   /   /

Code/Description/Expense

DAILY TOTAL

Tuesday   /   /

Code/Description/Expense

DAILY TOTAL

Wednesday   /   /

Code/Description/Expense

DAILY TOTAL

Thursday   /   /

Code/Description/Expense

DAILY TOTAL

Friday   /   /

Code/Description/Expense

DAILY TOTAL

Saturday   /   /

Code/Description/Expense

DAILY TOTAL

Sunday   /   /

Code/Description/Expense

DAILY TOTAL

WEEKLY SUMMARY — Week of _____ / _____ / _____

Weekly Total of Expenses (Add Daily Totals)

My Expenses _____ + Partner Expenses _____

Total _____

Actual Average Daily Total of Expenses
(Weekly Total of Expenses ÷ 7) _____

Under (+)/Over (-) Budget per day
(DDI Goal minus Actual Average
Daily Total of Expenses) _____

DDI GOAL IS $ _____

Monday	/	/
Code/Description/Expense		
DAILY TOTAL		

Tuesday	/	/
Code/Description/Expense		
DAILY TOTAL		

Wednesday	/	/
Code/Description/Expense		
DAILY TOTAL		

Thursday	/	/
Code/Description/Expense		
DAILY TOTAL		

Friday   /   /

Code/Description/Expense

DAILY TOTAL

Saturday   /   /

Code/Description/Expense

DAILY TOTAL

Sunday   /   /

Code/Description/Expense

DAILY TOTAL

WEEKLY SUMMARY — Week of _____ / _____ / _____

Weekly Total of Expenses (Add Daily Totals)

My Expenses _____ + Partner Expenses _____

Total _____

Actual Average Daily Total of Expenses
(Weekly Total of Expenses ÷ 7) _____

Under (+)/Over (-) Budget per day
(DDI Goal minus Actual Average
Daily Total of Expenses) _____

DDI GOAL IS $ _____

Monday   /   /

Code/Description/Expense

DAILY TOTAL

Tuesday   /   /

Code/Description/Expense

DAILY TOTAL

Wednesday   /   /

Code/Description/Expense

DAILY TOTAL

Thursday   /   /

Code/Description/Expense

DAILY TOTAL

Friday / /

Code/Description/Expense

DAILY TOTAL

Saturday / /

Code/Description/Expense

DAILY TOTAL

Sunday / /

Code/Description/Expense

DAILY TOTAL

WEEKLY SUMMARY — Week of _____ / _____ / _____

Weekly Total of Expenses (Add Daily Totals)

My Expenses _____ + Partner Expenses _____

Total _____

Actual Average Daily Total of Expenses
(Weekly Total of Expenses ÷ 7)   _____

Under (+)/Over (-) Budget per day
(DDI Goal minus Actual Average
Daily Total of Expenses)   _____

DDI GOAL IS $ _____

Monday / /

Code/Description/Expense

DAILY TOTAL

Tuesday / /

Code/Description/Expense

DAILY TOTAL

Wednesday / /

Code/Description/Expense

DAILY TOTAL

Thursday / /

Code/Description/Expense

DAILY TOTAL

Friday / /

Code/Description/Expense

DAILY TOTAL

Saturday / /

Code/Description/Expense

DAILY TOTAL

Sunday / /

Code/Description/Expense

DAILY TOTAL

WEEKLY SUMMARY — Week of ____ / ____ / ____

Weekly Total of Expenses (Add Daily Totals)

My Expenses _____ + Partner Expenses _____

Total _____

Actual Average Daily Total of Expenses
(Weekly Total of Expenses ÷ 7) _____

Under (+)/Over (-) Budget per day
(DDI Goal minus Actual Average
Daily Total of Expenses) _____

DDI GOAL IS $ _____

Monday	/	/

Code/Description/Expense

DAILY TOTAL

Tuesday	/	/

Code/Description/Expense

DAILY TOTAL

Wednesday	/	/

Code/Description/Expense

DAILY TOTAL

Thursday	/	/

Code/Description/Expense

DAILY TOTAL

Friday   /   /

Code/Description/Expense

DAILY TOTAL

Saturday   /   /

Code/Description/Expense

DAILY TOTAL

Sunday   /   /

Code/Description/Expense

DAILY TOTAL

WEEKLY SUMMARY — Week of _____ / _____ / _____

Weekly Total of Expenses (Add Daily Totals)
       My Expenses _____ + Partner Expenses _____
                                        Total _____

       Actual Average Daily Total of Expenses
       (Weekly Total of Expenses ÷ 7)   _____

       Under (+)/Over (-) Budget per day
       (DDI Goal minus Actual Average
       Daily Total of Expenses)   _____

DDI GOAL IS $ _____

Monday	/	/

Code/Description/Expense

DAILY TOTAL

Tuesday	/	/

Code/Description/Expense

DAILY TOTAL

Wednesday	/	/

Code/Description/Expense

DAILY TOTAL

Thursday	/	/

Code/Description/Expense

DAILY TOTAL

Friday / /

Code/Description/Expense

DAILY TOTAL

Saturday / /

Code/Description/Expense

DAILY TOTAL

Sunday / /

Code/Description/Expense

DAILY TOTAL

WEEKLY SUMMARY — Week of _____ / _____ / _____

Weekly Total of Expenses (Add Daily Totals)

My Expenses _____ + Partner Expenses _____

Total _____

Actual Average Daily Total of Expenses
(Weekly Total of Expenses ÷ 7) _____

Under (+)/Over (-) Budget per day
(DDI Goal minus Actual Average
Daily Total of Expenses) _____

DDI GOAL IS $ _____

Monday	/	/

Code/Description/Expense

DAILY TOTAL

Tuesday	/	/

Code/Description/Expense

DAILY TOTAL

Wednesday	/	/

Code/Description/Expense

DAILY TOTAL

Thursday	/	/

Code/Description/Expense

DAILY TOTAL

Friday   /   /

Code/Description/Expense

DAILY TOTAL

Saturday   /   /

Code/Description/Expense

DAILY TOTAL

Sunday   /   /

Code/Description/Expense

DAILY TOTAL

WEEKLY SUMMARY — Week of _____ / _____ / _____

Weekly Total of Expenses (Add Daily Totals)
       My Expenses _____ + Partner Expenses _____
                                      Total _____

       Actual Average Daily Total of Expenses
       (Weekly Total of Expenses ÷ 7)   _____

       Under (+)/Over (-) Budget per day
       (DDI Goal minus Actual Average
       Daily Total of Expenses)   _____

DDI GOAL IS $ _____

Monday / /

Code/Description/Expense

DAILY TOTAL

Tuesday / /

Code/Description/Expense

DAILY TOTAL

Wednesday / /

Code/Description/Expense

DAILY TOTAL

Thursday / /

Code/Description/Expense

DAILY TOTAL

Friday / /

Code/Description/Expense

DAILY TOTAL

Saturday / /

Code/Description/Expense

DAILY TOTAL

Sunday / /

Code/Description/Expense

DAILY TOTAL

WEEKLY SUMMARY — Week of _____ / _____ / _____

Weekly Total of Expenses (Add Daily Totals)

My Expenses _____ + Partner Expenses _____

Total _____

Actual Average Daily Total of Expenses
(Weekly Total of Expenses ÷ 7) _____

Under (+)/Over (-) Budget per day
(DDI Goal minus Actual Average
Daily Total of Expenses) _____

DDI GOAL IS $ _____

Monday / /

Code/Description/Expense

DAILY TOTAL

Tuesday / /

Code/Description/Expense

DAILY TOTAL

Wednesday / /

Code/Description/Expense

DAILY TOTAL

Thursday / /

Code/Description/Expense

DAILY TOTAL

Friday   /   /

Code/Description/Expense

DAILY TOTAL

Saturday   /   /

Code/Description/Expense

DAILY TOTAL

Sunday   /   /

Code/Description/Expense

DAILY TOTAL

WEEKLY SUMMARY — Week of _____ / _____ / _____

Weekly Total of Expenses (Add Daily Totals)

         My Expenses _____ + Partner Expenses _____

                                 Total _____

         Actual Average Daily Total of Expenses

         (Weekly Total of Expenses ÷ 7)   _____

         Under (+)/Over (-) Budget per day

         (DDI Goal minus Actual Average

         Daily Total of Expenses)   _____

DDI GOAL IS $ _____

Monday	/	/	

Code/Description/Expense

DAILY TOTAL

Tuesday	/	/	

Code/Description/Expense

DAILY TOTAL

Wednesday	/	/	

Code/Description/Expense

DAILY TOTAL

Thursday	/	/	

Code/Description/Expense

DAILY TOTAL

Friday   /   /

Code/Description/Expense

DAILY TOTAL

Saturday   /   /

Code/Description/Expense

DAILY TOTAL

Sunday   /   /

Code/Description/Expense

DAILY TOTAL

WEEKLY SUMMARY — Week of _____ / _____ / _____

Weekly Total of Expenses (Add Daily Totals)

My Expenses _____ + Partner Expenses _____

Total _____

Actual Average Daily Total of Expenses
(Weekly Total of Expenses ÷ 7) _____

Under (+)/Over (-) Budget per day
(DDI Goal minus Actual Average
Daily Total of Expenses) _____

DDI GOAL IS $ _____

Monday	/	/

Code/Description/Expense

DAILY TOTAL

Tuesday	/	/

Code/Description/Expense

DAILY TOTAL

Wednesday	/	/

Code/Description/Expense

DAILY TOTAL

Thursday	/	/

Code/Description/Expense

DAILY TOTAL

Friday   /   /

Code/Description/Expense

DAILY TOTAL

Saturday   /   /

Code/Description/Expense

DAILY TOTAL

Sunday   /   /

Code/Description/Expense

DAILY TOTAL

WEEKLY SUMMARY — Week of _____ / _____ / _____

Weekly Total of Expenses (Add Daily Totals)
        My Expenses _____ + Partner Expenses _____
                                                Total _____

        Actual Average Daily Total of Expenses
        (Weekly Total of Expenses ÷ 7)   _____

        Under (+)/Over (-) Budget per day
        (DDI Goal minus Actual Average
        Daily Total of Expenses)   _____

DDI GOAL IS $ _____

Monday   /   /

Code/Description/Expense

DAILY TOTAL

Tuesday   /   /

Code/Description/Expense

DAILY TOTAL

Wednesday   /   /

Code/Description/Expense

DAILY TOTAL

Thursday   /   /

Code/Description/Expense

DAILY TOTAL

Friday / /

Code/Description/Expense

DAILY TOTAL

Saturday / /

Code/Description/Expense

DAILY TOTAL

Sunday / /

Code/Description/Expense

DAILY TOTAL

WEEKLY SUMMARY — Week of ____ / ____ / ____

Weekly Total of Expenses (Add Daily Totals)

My Expenses _____ + Partner Expenses _____

Total _____

Actual Average Daily Total of Expenses
(Weekly Total of Expenses ÷ 7) _____

Under (+)/Over (-) Budget per day
(DDI Goal minus Actual Average
Daily Total of Expenses) _____

DDI GOAL IS $ _____

Monday	/	/	

Code/Description/Expense

DAILY TOTAL

Tuesday	/	/	

Code/Description/Expense

DAILY TOTAL

Wednesday	/	/	

Code/Description/Expense

DAILY TOTAL

Thursday	/	/	

Code/Description/Expense

DAILY TOTAL

Friday / /

Code/Description/Expense

DAILY TOTAL

Saturday / /

Code/Description/Expense

DAILY TOTAL

Sunday / /

Code/Description/Expense

DAILY TOTAL

WEEKLY SUMMARY — Week of _____ / _____ / _____

Weekly Total of Expenses (Add Daily Totals)
My Expenses _____ + Partner Expenses _____
Total _____

Actual Average Daily Total of Expenses
(Weekly Total of Expenses ÷ 7) _____

Under (+)/Over (-) Budget per day
(DDI Goal minus Actual Average
Daily Total of Expenses) _____

DDI GOAL IS $ _____

Monday	/	/	

Code/Description/Expense

DAILY TOTAL

Tuesday	/	/	

Code/Description/Expense

DAILY TOTAL

Wednesday	/	/	

Code/Description/Expense

DAILY TOTAL

Thursday	/	/	

Code/Description/Expense

DAILY TOTAL

Friday ___ / ___ / ___

Code/Description/Expense

DAILY TOTAL

Saturday ___ / ___ / ___

Code/Description/Expense

DAILY TOTAL

Sunday ___ / ___ / ___

Code/Description/Expense

DAILY TOTAL

WEEKLY SUMMARY — Week of ___ / ___ / ___

Weekly Total of Expenses (Add Daily Totals)
My Expenses _____ + Partner Expenses _____
Total _____

Actual Average Daily Total of Expenses
(Weekly Total of Expenses ÷ 7) _____

Under (+)/Over (-) Budget per day
(DDI Goal minus Actual Average
Daily Total of Expenses) _____

DDI GOAL IS $ _____

Monday	/	/

Code/Description/Expense

 DAILY TOTAL

Tuesday	/	/

Code/Description/Expense

 DAILY TOTAL

Wednesday	/	/

Code/Description/Expense

 DAILY TOTAL

Thursday	/	/

Code/Description/Expense

 DAILY TOTAL

Friday   /   /

Code/Description/Expense

DAILY TOTAL

Saturday   /   /

Code/Description/Expense

DAILY TOTAL

Sunday   /   /

Code/Description/Expense

DAILY TOTAL

WEEKLY SUMMARY — Week of _____ / _____ / _____

Weekly Total of Expenses (Add Daily Totals)

My Expenses _____ + Partner Expenses _____

Total _____

Actual Average Daily Total of Expenses
(Weekly Total of Expenses ÷ 7)   _____

Under (+)/Over (-) Budget per day
(DDI Goal minus Actual Average
Daily Total of Expenses)   _____

DDI GOAL IS $ _____

Monday	/	/

Code/Description/Expense

DAILY TOTAL

Tuesday	/	/

Code/Description/Expense

DAILY TOTAL

Wednesday	/	/

Code/Description/Expense

DAILY TOTAL

Thursday	/	/

Code/Description/Expense

DAILY TOTAL

Friday   /   /

Code/Description/Expense

DAILY TOTAL

Saturday   /   /

Code/Description/Expense

DAILY TOTAL

Sunday   /   /

Code/Description/Expense

DAILY TOTAL

WEEKLY SUMMARY — Week of _____ / _____ / _____

Weekly Total of Expenses (Add Daily Totals)

My Expenses _____ + Partner Expenses _____

Total _____

Actual Average Daily Total of Expenses
(Weekly Total of Expenses ÷ 7) _____

Under (+)/Over (-) Budget per day
(DDI Goal minus Actual Average
Daily Total of Expenses) _____

DDI GOAL IS $ _____

Monday	/	/

Code/Description/Expense

_____
_____
_____
_____
_____

DAILY TOTAL

Tuesday	/	/

Code/Description/Expense

_____
_____
_____
_____
_____

DAILY TOTAL

Wednesday	/	/

Code/Description/Expense

_____
_____
_____
_____
_____

DAILY TOTAL

Thursday	/	/

Code/Description/Expense

_____
_____
_____
_____

DAILY TOTAL

Friday   /   /

Code/Description/Expense

DAILY TOTAL

Saturday   /   /

Code/Description/Expense

DAILY TOTAL

Sunday   /   /

Code/Description/Expense

DAILY TOTAL

WEEKLY SUMMARY — Week of _____ / _____ / _____

Weekly Total of Expenses (Add Daily Totals)

     My Expenses _____ + Partner Expenses _____

                                          Total _____

     Actual Average Daily Total of Expenses

     (Weekly Total of Expenses ÷ 7)   _____

     Under (+)/Over (-) Budget per day

     (DDI Goal minus Actual Average

     Daily Total of Expenses)   _____

DDI GOAL IS $ _____

Monday	/	/

Code/Description/Expense

DAILY TOTAL

Tuesday	/	/

Code/Description/Expense

DAILY TOTAL

Wednesday	/	/

Code/Description/Expense

DAILY TOTAL

Thursday	/	/

Code/Description/Expense

DAILY TOTAL

Friday   /   /

Code/Description/Expense

DAILY TOTAL

Saturday   /   /

Code/Description/Expense

DAILY TOTAL

Sunday   /   /

Code/Description/Expense

DAILY TOTAL

WEEKLY SUMMARY — Week of _____ / _____ / _____

Weekly Total of Expenses (Add Daily Totals)

         My Expenses _____ + Partner Expenses _____

                                         Total _____

         Actual Average Daily Total of Expenses

         (Weekly Total of Expenses ÷ 7)   _____

         Under (+)/Over (-) Budget per day

         (DDI Goal minus Actual Average

         Daily Total of Expenses)   _____

DDI GOAL IS $ _____

Monday   /   /

Code/Description/Expense

DAILY TOTAL

Tuesday   /   /

Code/Description/Expense

DAILY TOTAL

Wednesday   /   /

Code/Description/Expense

DAILY TOTAL

Thursday   /   /

Code/Description/Expense

DAILY TOTAL

Friday   /   /

Code/Description/Expense

DAILY TOTAL

Saturday   /   /

Code/Description/Expense

DAILY TOTAL

Sunday   /   /

Code/Description/Expense

DAILY TOTAL

WEEKLY SUMMARY — Week of _____ / _____ / _____

Weekly Total of Expenses (Add Daily Totals)

My Expenses _____ + Partner Expenses _____

Total _____

Actual Average Daily Total of Expenses
(Weekly Total of Expenses ÷ 7) _____

Under (+)/Over (-) Budget per day
(DDI Goal minus Actual Average
Daily Total of Expenses) _____

DDI GOAL IS $ _____

Monday	/	/

Code/Description/Expense

DAILY TOTAL

Tuesday	/	/

Code/Description/Expense

DAILY TOTAL

Wednesday	/	/

Code/Description/Expense

DAILY TOTAL

Thursday	/	/

Code/Description/Expense

DAILY TOTAL

Friday ___/___/___

Code/Description/Expense

DAILY TOTAL

Saturday ___/___/___

Code/Description/Expense

DAILY TOTAL

Sunday ___/___/___

Code/Description/Expense

DAILY TOTAL

WEEKLY SUMMARY — Week of ____/____/____

Weekly Total of Expenses (Add Daily Totals)

My Expenses _____ + Partner Expenses _____

Total _____

Actual Average Daily Total of Expenses
(Weekly Total of Expenses ÷ 7) _____

Under (+)/Over (-) Budget per day
(DDI Goal minus Actual Average
Daily Total of Expenses) _____

DDI GOAL IS $ _____

Monday	/	/
Code/Description/Expense		
DAILY TOTAL		

Tuesday	/	/
Code/Description/Expense		
DAILY TOTAL		

Wednesday	/	/
Code/Description/Expense		
DAILY TOTAL		

Thursday	/	/
Code/Description/Expense		
DAILY TOTAL		

Friday / /

Code/Description/Expense

DAILY TOTAL

Saturday / /

Code/Description/Expense

DAILY TOTAL

Sunday / /

Code/Description/Expense

DAILY TOTAL

WEEKLY SUMMARY — Week of _____ / _____ / _____

Weekly Total of Expenses (Add Daily Totals)

    My Expenses _____ + Partner Expenses _____

                                  Total _____

    Actual Average Daily Total of Expenses

    (Weekly Total of Expenses ÷ 7) _____

    Under (+)/Over (-) Budget per day

    (DDI Goal minus Actual Average

    Daily Total of Expenses) _____

DDI GOAL IS $ _____

Monday / /

Code/Description/Expense

DAILY TOTAL

Tuesday / /

Code/Description/Expense

DAILY TOTAL

Wednesday / /

Code/Description/Expense

DAILY TOTAL

Thursday / /

Code/Description/Expense

DAILY TOTAL

Friday / /

Code/Description/Expense

DAILY TOTAL

Saturday / /

Code/Description/Expense

DAILY TOTAL

Sunday / /

Code/Description/Expense

DAILY TOTAL

WEEKLY SUMMARY — Week of _____ / _____ / _____

Weekly Total of Expenses (Add Daily Totals)

My Expenses _____ + Partner Expenses _____

Total _____

Actual Average Daily Total of Expenses

(Weekly Total of Expenses ÷ 7) _____

Under (+)/Over (-) Budget per day

(DDI Goal minus Actual Average

Daily Total of Expenses) _____

DDI GOAL IS $ _____

Monday / /

Code/Description/Expense

DAILY TOTAL

Tuesday / /

Code/Description/Expense

DAILY TOTAL

Wednesday / /

Code/Description/Expense

DAILY TOTAL

Thursday / /

Code/Description/Expense

DAILY TOTAL

Friday / /

Code/Description/Expense

DAILY TOTAL

Saturday / /

Code/Description/Expense

DAILY TOTAL

Sunday / /

Code/Description/Expense

DAILY TOTAL

WEEKLY SUMMARY — Week of _____ / _____ / _____

Weekly Total of Expenses (Add Daily Totals)

My Expenses _____ + Partner Expenses _____

Total _____

Actual Average Daily Total of Expenses
(Weekly Total of Expenses ÷ 7) _____

Under (+)/Over (-) Budget per day
(DDI Goal minus Actual Average
Daily Total of Expenses) _____

DDI GOAL IS

$ _____

Monday	/	/

Code/Description/Expense

DAILY TOTAL

Tuesday	/	/

Code/Description/Expense

DAILY TOTAL

Wednesday	/	/

Code/Description/Expense

DAILY TOTAL

Thursday	/	/

Code/Description/Expense

DAILY TOTAL

Friday / /

Code/Description/Expense

DAILY TOTAL

Saturday / /

Code/Description/Expense

DAILY TOTAL

Sunday / /

Code/Description/Expense

DAILY TOTAL

WEEKLY SUMMARY — Week of _____ / _____ / _____

Weekly Total of Expenses (Add Daily Totals)

My Expenses _____ + Partner Expenses _____

Total _____

Actual Average Daily Total of Expenses
(Weekly Total of Expenses ÷ 7) _____

Under (+)/Over (-) Budget per day
(DDI Goal minus Actual Average
Daily Total of Expenses) _____

DDI GOAL IS $ _____

Monday   /   /

Code/Description/Expense

DAILY TOTAL

Tuesday   /   /

Code/Description/Expense

DAILY TOTAL

Wednesday   /   /

Code/Description/Expense

DAILY TOTAL

Thursday   /   /

Code/Description/Expense

DAILY TOTAL

Friday / /

Code/Description/Expense

DAILY TOTAL

Saturday / /

Code/Description/Expense

DAILY TOTAL

Sunday / /

Code/Description/Expense

DAILY TOTAL

WEEKLY SUMMARY — Week of _____ / _____ / _____

Weekly Total of Expenses (Add Daily Totals)
  My Expenses _____ + Partner Expenses _____
                                                    Total _____

  Actual Average Daily Total of Expenses
  (Weekly Total of Expenses ÷ 7) _____

  Under (+)/Over (-) Budget per day
  (DDI Goal minus Actual Average
  Daily Total of Expenses) _____

DDI GOAL IS $ _____

Monday	/	/

Code/Description/Expense

DAILY TOTAL

Tuesday	/	/

Code/Description/Expense

DAILY TOTAL

Wednesday	/	/

Code/Description/Expense

DAILY TOTAL

Thursday	/	/

Code/Description/Expense

DAILY TOTAL

Friday / /

Code/Description/Expense

DAILY TOTAL

Saturday / /

Code/Description/Expense

DAILY TOTAL

Sunday / /

Code/Description/Expense

DAILY TOTAL

WEEKLY SUMMARY — Week of _____ / _____ / _____

Weekly Total of Expenses (Add Daily Totals)

My Expenses _____ + Partner Expenses _____

Total _____

Actual Average Daily Total of Expenses
(Weekly Total of Expenses ÷ 7) _____

Under (+)/Over (-) Budget per day
(DDI Goal minus Actual Average
Daily Total of Expenses) _____

DDI GOAL IS $ _____

Monday	/	/

Code/Description/Expense

DAILY TOTAL

Tuesday	/	/

Code/Description/Expense

DAILY TOTAL

Wednesday	/	/

Code/Description/Expense

DAILY TOTAL

Thursday	/	/

Code/Description/Expense

DAILY TOTAL

Friday   /   /

Code/Description/Expense

DAILY TOTAL

Saturday   /   /

Code/Description/Expense

DAILY TOTAL

Sunday   /   /

Code/Description/Expense

DAILY TOTAL

WEEKLY SUMMARY — Week of _____ / _____ / _____

Weekly Total of Expenses (Add Daily Totals)

My Expenses _____ + Partner Expenses _____

Total _____

Actual Average Daily Total of Expenses
(Weekly Total of Expenses ÷ 7)   _____

Under (+)/Over (-) Budget per day
(DDI Goal minus Actual Average
Daily Total of Expenses)   _____

DDI GOAL IS $ _____

Monday	/	/
Code/Description/Expense		
DAILY TOTAL		

Tuesday	/	/
Code/Description/Expense		
DAILY TOTAL		

Wednesday	/	/
Code/Description/Expense		
DAILY TOTAL		

Thursday	/	/
Code/Description/Expense		
DAILY TOTAL		

Friday / /

Code/Description/Expense

DAILY TOTAL

Saturday / /

Code/Description/Expense

DAILY TOTAL

Sunday / /

Code/Description/Expense

DAILY TOTAL

WEEKLY SUMMARY — Week of ____ / ____ / ____

Weekly Total of Expenses (Add Daily Totals)

My Expenses _____ + Partner Expenses _____

Total _____

Actual Average Daily Total of Expenses
(Weekly Total of Expenses ÷ 7)   _____

Under (+)/Over (-) Budget per day
(DDI Goal minus Actual Average
Daily Total of Expenses)   _____

DDI GOAL IS $ _____

Monday	/	/

Code/Description/Expense

DAILY TOTAL

Tuesday	/	/

Code/Description/Expense

DAILY TOTAL

Wednesday	/	/

Code/Description/Expense

DAILY TOTAL

Thursday	/	/

Code/Description/Expense

DAILY TOTAL

Friday   /   /

Code/Description/Expense

DAILY TOTAL

Saturday   /   /

Code/Description/Expense

DAILY TOTAL

Sunday   /   /

Code/Description/Expense

DAILY TOTAL

WEEKLY SUMMARY — Week of _____ / _____ / _____

Weekly Total of Expenses (Add Daily Totals)

     My Expenses _____ + Partner Expenses _____

                                    Total _____

     Actual Average Daily Total of Expenses

     (Weekly Total of Expenses ÷ 7)   _____

     Under (+)/Over (-) Budget per day

     (DDI Goal minus Actual Average

     Daily Total of Expenses)   _____

DDI GOAL IS $ _____

| **Monday** | / | / | |

Code/Description/Expense

DAILY TOTAL

| **Tuesday** | / | / | |

Code/Description/Expense

DAILY TOTAL

| **Wednesday** | / | / | |

Code/Description/Expense

DAILY TOTAL

| **Thursday** | / | / | |

Code/Description/Expense

DAILY TOTAL

Friday   /   /

Code/Description/Expense

DAILY TOTAL

Saturday   /   /

Code/Description/Expense

DAILY TOTAL

Sunday   /   /

Code/Description/Expense

DAILY TOTAL

WEEKLY SUMMARY — Week of _____ / _____ / _____

Weekly Total of Expenses (Add Daily Totals)

My Expenses _____ + Partner Expenses _____

Total _____

Actual Average Daily Total of Expenses
(Weekly Total of Expenses ÷ 7) _____

Under (+)/Over (-) Budget per day
(DDI Goal minus Actual Average
Daily Total of Expenses) _____

DDI GOAL IS $ _____

Monday	/	/

Code/Description/Expense

DAILY TOTAL

Tuesday	/	/

Code/Description/Expense

DAILY TOTAL

Wednesday	/	/

Code/Description/Expense

DAILY TOTAL

Thursday	/	/

Code/Description/Expense

DAILY TOTAL

Friday / /

Code/Description/Expense

DAILY TOTAL

Saturday / /

Code/Description/Expense

DAILY TOTAL

Sunday / /

Code/Description/Expense

DAILY TOTAL

WEEKLY SUMMARY — Week of _____ / _____ / _____

Weekly Total of Expenses (Add Daily Totals)
           My Expenses _____ + Partner Expenses _____
                                                    Total _____

           Actual Average Daily Total of Expenses
           (Weekly Total of Expenses ÷ 7)   _____

           Under (+)/Over (-) Budget per day
           (DDI Goal minus Actual Average
           Daily Total of Expenses)   _____

DDI GOAL IS $ _____

Monday	/	/

Code/Description/Expense

DAILY TOTAL

Tuesday	/	/

Code/Description/Expense

DAILY TOTAL

Wednesday	/	/

Code/Description/Expense

DAILY TOTAL

Thursday	/	/

Code/Description/Expense

DAILY TOTAL

Friday / /

Code/Description/Expense

DAILY TOTAL

Saturday / /

Code/Description/Expense

DAILY TOTAL

Sunday / /

Code/Description/Expense

DAILY TOTAL

WEEKLY SUMMARY — Week of _____ / _____ / _____

Weekly Total of Expenses (Add Daily Totals)

My Expenses _____ + Partner Expenses _____

Total _____

Actual Average Daily Total of Expenses
(Weekly Total of Expenses ÷ 7)   _____

Under (+)/Over (-) Budget per day
(DDI Goal minus Actual Average
Daily Total of Expenses)   _____

DDI GOAL IS $ _____

Monday	/	/	

Code/Description/Expense

DAILY TOTAL

Tuesday	/	/	

Code/Description/Expense

DAILY TOTAL

Wednesday	/	/	

Code/Description/Expense

DAILY TOTAL

Thursday	/	/	

Code/Description/Expense

DAILY TOTAL

Friday   /   /

Code/Description/Expense

DAILY TOTAL

Saturday   /   /

Code/Description/Expense

DAILY TOTAL

Sunday   /   /

Code/Description/Expense

DAILY TOTAL

WEEKLY SUMMARY — Week of _____ / _____ / _____

Weekly Total of Expenses (Add Daily Totals)

My Expenses _____ + Partner Expenses _____

Total _____

Actual Average Daily Total of Expenses
(Weekly Total of Expenses ÷ 7) _____

Under (+)/Over (-) Budget per day
(DDI Goal minus Actual Average
Daily Total of Expenses) _____

DDI GOAL IS $ _____

Monday	/	/	

Code/Description/Expense

DAILY TOTAL

Tuesday	/	/	

Code/Description/Expense

DAILY TOTAL

Wednesday	/	/	

Code/Description/Expense

DAILY TOTAL

Thursday	/	/	

Code/Description/Expense

DAILY TOTAL

Friday ___ / ___ /

Code/Description/Expense

DAILY TOTAL

Saturday ___ / ___ /

Code/Description/Expense

DAILY TOTAL

Sunday ___ / ___ /

Code/Description/Expense

DAILY TOTAL

WEEKLY SUMMARY — Week of ___ / ___ / ___

Weekly Total of Expenses (Add Daily Totals)

My Expenses _____ + Partner Expenses _____

Total _____

Actual Average Daily Total of Expenses
(Weekly Total of Expenses ÷ 7) _____

Under (+)/Over (-) Budget per day
(DDI Goal minus Actual Average
Daily Total of Expenses) _____

BUDGET
SUMMARIES
MONTHLY - QUARTERLY

Monthly Budget Summary

JANUARY

Monthly Total of Expenses *

(Add Daily Totals of Expenses for January) $ _____

Actual Average Per Day

(Monthly Total of Expenses ÷ number of days in the month) $ _____

DDI ** Goal

$ _____

Under (+)/Over (-) Budget Per Day

(DDI Goal minus Actual Average Expense Per Day) $ _____

x 365 = Projected Year End Surplus/Deficit

$ _____

How can I improve?

_____

_____

_____

_____

_____

* Expenses other than Fixed and Semi-Fixed Expenses

** Daily Disposable Income

Monthly Budget Summary

FEBRUARY

Monthly Total of Expenses *

(Add Daily Totals of Expenses for February) $ _____

Actual Average Per Day

(Monthly Total of Expenses ÷ number of days in the month) $ _____

DDI ** Goal

$ _____

Under (+)/Over (-) Budget Per Day

(DDI Goal minus Actual Average Expense Per Day) $ _____

x 365 = Projected Year End Surplus/Deficit

$ _____

How can I improve?

_____

_____

_____

_____

_____

* Expenses other than Fixed and Semi-Fixed Expenses

** Daily Disposable Income

Monthly Budget Summary

MARCH

Monthly Total of Expenses *

(Add Daily Totals of Expenses for March) $ _____

Actual Average Per Day

(Monthly Total of Expenses ÷ number of days in the month) $ _____

DDI ** Goal

$ _____

Under (+)/Over (-) Budget Per Day

(DDI Goal minus Actual Average Expense Per Day) $ _____

x 365 = Projected Year End Surplus/Deficit

$ _____

How can I improve?

_____

_____

_____

_____

_____

* Expenses other than Fixed and Semi-Fixed Expenses

** Daily Disposable Income

Monthly Budget Summary

APRIL

Monthly Total of Expenses *

(Add Daily Totals of Expenses for April) $ _____

Actual Average Per Day

(Monthly Total of Expenses ÷ number of days in the month) $ _____

DDI ** Goal

$ _____

Under (+)/Over (-) Budget Per Day

(DDI Goal minus Actual Average Expense Per Day) $ _____

x 365 = Projected Year End Surplus/Deficit

$ _____

How can I improve?

_____

_____

_____

_____

_____

* Expenses other than Fixed and Semi-Fixed Expenses

** Daily Disposable Income

Monthly Budget Summary

MAY

Monthly Total of Expenses *	
(Add Daily Totals of Expenses for May)	$

Actual Average Per Day	
(Monthly Total of Expenses ÷ number of days in the month)	$

DDI ** Goal	
	$

Under (+)/Over (-) Budget Per Day	
(DDI Goal minus Actual Average Expense Per Day)	$

x 365 = Projected Year End Surplus/Deficit	
	$

How can I improve?

_____

_____

_____

_____

_____

* Expenses other than Fixed and Semi-Fixed Expenses

** Daily Disposable Income

Monthly Budget Summary

JUNE

Monthly Total of Expenses *

(Add Daily Totals of Expenses for June) $ _____

Actual Average Per Day

(Monthly Total of Expenses ÷ number of days in the month) $ _____

DDI ** Goal

$ _____

Under (+)/Over (-) Budget Per Day

(DDI Goal minus Actual Average Expense Per Day) $ _____

x 365 = Projected Year End Surplus/Deficit

$ _____

How can I improve?

_____

_____

_____

_____

_____

* Expenses other than Fixed and Semi-Fixed Expenses
** Daily Disposable Income

Monthly Budget Summary

JULY

Monthly Total of Expenses *

(Add Daily Totals of Expenses for July) $ _____

Actual Average Per Day

(Monthly Total of Expenses ÷ number of days in the month) $ _____

DDI ** Goal

                                                                 $ _____

Under (+)/Over (-) Budget Per Day

(DDI Goal minus Actual Average Expense Per Day) $ _____

x 365 = Projected Year End Surplus/Deficit

                                                                 $ _____

How can I improve?

_____

_____

_____

_____

_____

* Expenses other than Fixed and Semi-Fixed Expenses

** Daily Disposable Income

Monthly Budget Summary

AUGUST

Monthly Total of Expenses *

(Add Daily Totals of Expenses for August) $ _____

Actual Average Per Day

(Monthly Total of Expenses ÷ number of days in the month) $ _____

DDI ** Goal

$ _____

Under (+)/Over (-) Budget Per Day

(DDI Goal minus Actual Average Expense Per Day) $ _____

x 365 = Projected Year End Surplus/Deficit

$ _____

How can I improve?

_____

_____

_____

_____

_____

* Expenses other than Fixed and Semi-Fixed Expenses

** Daily Disposable Income

Monthly Budget Summary

SEPTEMBER

Monthly Total of Expenses *

(Add Daily Totals of Expenses for September) $ _____

Actual Average Per Day

(Monthly Total of Expenses ÷ number of days in the month) $ _____

DDI ** Goal

$ _____

Under (+)/Over (-) Budget Per Day

(DDI Goal minus Actual Average Expense Per Day) $ _____

x 365 = Projected Year End Surplus/Deficit

$ _____

How can I improve?

_____

_____

_____

_____

_____

* Expenses other than Fixed and Semi-Fixed Expenses
** Daily Disposable Income

Monthly Budget Summary

OCTOBER

Monthly Total of Expenses *

(Add Daily Totals of Expenses for October) $ _____

Actual Average Per Day

(Monthly Total of Expenses ÷ number of days in the month) $ _____

DDI ** Goal

$ _____

Under (+)/Over (-) Budget Per Day

(DDI Goal minus Actual Average Expense Per Day) $ _____

x 365 = Projected Year End Surplus/Deficit

$ _____

How can I improve?

_____

_____

_____

_____

_____

* Expenses other than Fixed and Semi-Fixed Expenses

** Daily Disposable Income

Monthly Budget Summary

NOVEMBER

Monthly Total of Expenses *

(Add Daily Totals of Expenses for November)

$ _____

Actual Average Per Day

(Monthly Total of Expenses ÷ number of days in the month)

$ _____

DDI ** Goal

$ _____

Under (+)/Over (-) Budget Per Day

(DDI Goal minus Actual Average Expense Per Day)

$ _____

x 365 = Projected Year End Surplus/Deficit

$ _____

How can I improve?

_____

_____

_____

_____

_____

* Expenses other than Fixed and Semi-Fixed Expenses
** Daily Disposable Income

Monthly Budget Summary

DECEMBER

Monthly Total of Expenses *

(Add Daily Totals of Expenses for December) $ _____

Actual Average Per Day

(Monthly Total of Expenses ÷ number of days in the month) $ _____

DDI ** Goal

$ _____

Under (+)/Over (-) Budget Per Day

(DDI Goal minus Actual Average Expense Per Day) $ _____

x 365 = Projected Year End Surplus/Deficit

$ _____

How can I improve?

_____

_____

_____

_____

_____

* Expenses other than Fixed and Semi-Fixed Expenses

** Daily Disposable Income

Quarterly Budget Summary

JAN/FEB/MAR

Quarterly Total of Expenses *

(Add Monthly Totals of Expenses for Jan/Feb/Mar)　　　　　$ _____

Actual Average Per Day

(Quarterly Total of Expenses ÷ number of days in the quarter)　　$ _____

DDI ** Goal

$ _____

Under (+)/Over (-) Budget Per Day

(DDI Goal minus Actual Average Expense Per Day)　　　　$ _____

x 365 = Projected Year End Surplus/Deficit

$ _____

How can I improve?

_____

_____

_____

_____

_____

* Expenses other than Fixed and Semi-Fixed Expenses

** Daily Disposable Income

Quarterly Budget Summary

APR/MAY/JUN

Quarterly Total of Expenses *

(Add Monthly Totals of Expenses for Apr/May/Jun) $ _____

Actual Average Per Day

(Quarterly Total of Expenses ÷ number of days in the quarter) $ _____

DDI ** Goal

$ _____

Under (+)/Over (-) Budget Per Day

(DDI Goal minus Actual Average Expense Per Day) $ _____

x 365 = Projected Year End Surplus/Deficit

$ _____

How can I improve?

_____

_____

_____

_____

_____

* Expenses other than Fixed and Semi-Fixed Expenses

** Daily Disposable Income

Quarterly Budget Summary

JUL/AUG/SEPT

Quarterly Total of Expenses *

(Add Monthly Totals of Expenses for Jul/Aug/Sept)　　　　　　　$

Actual Average Per Day

(Quarterly Total of Expenses ÷ number of days in the quarter)　　$

DDI ** Goal

$

Under (+)/Over (-) Budget Per Day

(DDI Goal minus Actual Average Expense Per Day)　　　　　　$

x 365 = Projected Year End Surplus/Deficit

$

How can I improve?

_____

_____

_____

_____

_____

* Expenses other than Fixed and Semi-Fixed Expenses
** Daily Disposable Income

Quarterly Budget Summary

OCT/NOV/DEC

Quarterly Total of Expenses *

(Add Monthly Totals of Expenses for Oct/Nov/Dec) $ _____

Actual Average Per Day

(Quarterly Total of Expenses ÷ number of days in the quarter) $ _____

DDI ** Goal

$ _____

Under (+)/Over (-) Budget Per Day

(DDI Goal minus Actual Average Expense Per Day) $ _____

x 365 = Projected Year End Surplus/Deficit

$ _____

How can I improve?

_____

_____

_____

_____

_____

* Expenses other than Fixed and Semi-Fixed Expenses
** Daily Disposable Income

Yearly Budget Summary

Yearly Total of Expenses *

(Add Quarterly Totals of Expenses for the year) $ _____

Actual Average Per Day

(Yearly Total of Expenses ÷ 365) $ _____

DDI ** Goal

$ _____

Under (+)/Over (-) Budget Per Day

(DDI Goal minus Actual Average Expense Per Day) $ _____

x 365 = Projected Year End Surplus/Deficit

$ _____

How can I improve?

_____

_____

_____

_____

_____

* Expenses other than Fixed and Semi-Fixed Expenses

** Daily Disposable Income

NOTES

NOTES

RECOMMENDED READING

AND WEBSITES

David Bach, *The Automatic Millionaire: A Powerful One-Step Plan to Live and Finish Rich* (New York: Broadway Books, 2003).

Jean Chatzky, *The Ten Commandments of Financial Happiness: Feel Richer with What You've Got* (New York: Portfolio/Penguin Books, 2005).

Marla Cilley, *Sink Reflections* (New York: Bantam Books, 2002). FlyLady's successful system of conquering CHAOS and learning how to FLY (Finally Loving Yourself).

Leanne Ely, *Saving Dinner: The Menus, Recipes, and Shopping Lists to Bring Your Family Back to the Table* (New York: Ballantine Books, 2009).

Peter G. Peterson, *The Education of an American Dreamer* (New York: Twelve/Hachette Book Group, 2009).

Kevin Phillips, *American Theocracy: The Peril and Politics of Radical Religion, Oil, and Borrowed Money in the 21st Century* (New York: Viking, 2006).

Dave Ramsey, *The Money Answer Book* (Nashville, TN: Thomas Nelson, 2005).

Bob Sullivan, *Gotcha Capitalism: How Hidden Fees Rip You Off Every Day— And What You Can Do About It* (New York: Ballantine Books, 2007).

www.ewealthwatchers.com
www.flylady.net
www.bankrate.com
www.practicalmoneyskills.com
www.mymoney.gov

Recommended Reading and Websites

www.savingdinner.com
www.everydaycheapskate.com
www.mint.com
www.coupons.com
www.msgen.com

Go to the Visa website, especially the financial literacy page:
http://www.corporate.visa.com/

For a transcript of the NPR *Morning Edition* broadcast "Why We Spend More Using Credit Cards vs Cash":
http://www.npr.org/templates/story/story.php?storyId=92178034

For a global survey by Gallup measuring happiness around the world:
http://www.nytimes.com/imagepages/2008/04/16/business/20080416
_LEONHARDT_GRAPHIC.html

For a February 25, 2009, *Wall Street Journal* article on how cost of owning relative to renting has fallen since the housing bubble burst:
http://online.msj.com/article/SB123552129423664663.html

For credit score:
http://www.myfico.com/Default.aspx

INDEX

ABOUT THE AUTHOR

Alice Wood, a native of Naperville, Illinois, has spent much of the past twenty-five years working as an estate planning attorney. She has represented more than a thousand families throughout her career. In 2005 she launched Wealth Watchers International®, a movement dedicated to helping people spend less money than they make through the philosophy that *Every day and every dollar make a difference.*®